Women Are Always Right

and

Men Are Never Wrong

Joey O'Connor is a conference speaker and the author of ten books for couples, parents, and young adults. He lives with his wife and children in San Clemente, California, where he likes to surf, eat fish tacos, and lie in the hot sand.

His works include:

In His Steps: The Promise

You're Grounded for Life: And 49 Other Crazy Things Parents Say

Heaven's Not A Crying Place: Teaching Your Child about Funerals, Death, & the Life Beyond

Excuse Me! I'll Take My Piece of the Planet Now

Whadd'ya Gonna Do? 25 Steps for Getting a Life

Breaking Your Comfort Zones: And 49 Extremely Radical Ways to Live for God

Where is God When . . . 1001 Answers to Questions Students Are Asking

Graffiti for Gen X Guys by J. David Schmidt with Joey O'Connor

Graffiti for Gen X Girls by J. DAvid Schmidt with Joey O'Connor

For speaking events, conferences and seminars, please call (949) 369-6767. You can also write to Joey O'Connor at P.O. Box 3373, San Clemente, CA 92674-3373.

For more information about Joey O'Connor, visit Joey's web site: http//www.joeyo.com. You can email Joey with your comments and questions at: joey@joeyo.com

Women Are Always Right

and

Men Are Never Wrong

JOEY O'CONNOR

WORD PUBLISHING
NASHVILLE
A Thomas Nelson Company

Published by Word Publishing, Nashville, Tennessee.

Library of Congress Cataloging-in-Publication Data

O'Connor, Joey, 1964–
    Women are always right and men are never wrong / by Joey O'Connor.
      p. cm.
    ISBN 0-8499-3704-3
    1. Marriage—United States. 2. Communication in marriage—United States. 3. Man-Woman relationships—United States. I. Title.
HQ734.0295 1999
306.81—dc21

                                    98-45332
                                         CIP

Printed in the United States of America
99 00 01 02 03 04 QPV 9 8 7 6 5 4 3 2

To Krista,
the one who puts up
with all my extremes.

Contents

Introduction

*h*ouston, *we have a problem.*

That's how too many marriage books start. Sure, there are a lot of helpful marriage books on the market today, but some of them are way too serious. What about those books that start with one-hundred-question, multiple-choice marriage inventories? You think your marriage is going pretty well and you score a 95. Your spouse thinks differently, goes to the other extreme and scores a 57. What are you supposed to do then? Average your scores? I'm convinced that some marriage books are more work than marriage itself.

Take heart. We all know creating a good marriage is hard work, but in this book, I'm not going to force you to do or be anything you're not. Your job is to sit back, laugh, and take a few sips from the Diet Coke of marriage books. I hope you'll glean a few ideas that will be helpful for your marriage. Even better, this book won't give you the shakes. *It is caffeine-free.*

When I first started working on this book, Krista, my wife (who intimately knows that I would never, never, never, ever think of going to extremes), wanted me to title this book *Women Are Always Right . . . Period!* She thought I'd sell a lot more books that way.

I said, "No way, José."

My oldest daughter, Janae, accidentally thought the title of the book was *Men Are Always Wrong.* When I corrected her, she laughed and told me she liked her title better.

Am I lacking for ideas, opinions, or suggested title changes in my home or what? I don't know about you, your spouse, or your marriage, but every time my wife and I get into a spat, tiff, fight, disagreement, or, um, "polite discussion," it doesn't matter how right I am and how wrong Krista is, I always have to apologize. It doesn't matter if I'm the one who was napalmed, hurt, attacked, accused, or scarred for life, I always have to say I'm sorry for the mere existence of whatever we're fighting about.

Of course, most of the time, I am wrong. But don't misunderstand that as an admission of guilt. I concede that it's hard (okay, very difficult) for guys to admit when they're wrong, but it's easier to pull a top sirloin from a couple of snarling Dobermans than to get a woman to admit she's not always right. Forget this '70s era battle of the sexes stuff; until someone figures out once and for all who's always right and who's never wrong, we're talking war.

So here I am.

This is the last marriage book you'll ever need. At least until I write the next one. Not only will this book guarantee world peace, marital bliss, endless nights of sexual passion, and complete interpersonal harmony, it'll also serve as a good projectile when your husband or wife is bugging the heck out of you.

When I began working on this book, friends asked me what type of book I was writing. My response? "I'm working on a marriage book—a humor book." That comment alone set 'em off. Boy, did I get an earful. I hit the Marriage Mother Lode. I had numerous individuals asking me if I needed a coauthor for the book, quips about male/female idiosyncrasies, moans and groans, jokes about men being La-Z-Boy lugheads who can't put the kids to bed without inciting a riot, female jokes about shopping, shopping, and PMS. And sex. I learned very quickly that men and women have strong opinions about marriage.

This book is about the basics of love and marriage, the fundamental elements of honor, respect, communication, wants, needs, desires, honesty, cooperation, and forgiveness in marriage. What matters most here is not my opinion, but how you and your spouse laugh and learn about the extremes you are prone to in your marriage.

Inside you'll find plenty of humorous marriage stories, yes, the naked truth of what really happens in every marriage, the sparks that fly, the wild blustery posturing, and not-so-far-from-the-truth hypothetical scenarios of the crazy extremes you and your spouse resort to just to get each other's attention. If you and I are going to rant and rave when we go to extremes, let's at least learn to laugh at ourselves when we're finished with all our huffing and puffing.

I'm convinced that if you and your spouse work on the basic elements of your marriage, then you can create a great marriage together. Finding common ground in your marriage is all about working on the basics and learning not to make those periodic extremes a way of life.

Marriage isn't rocket science, but too many extremes can veer any marriage off course. Do the basics very well and shoot high for making your marriage the very best it can be. Do that and you'll be able to say with confidence, "Houston, we have liftoff."

Hurry Up, We're Going to Be Late

1

Where's the real stuff in life to cling to?
Love is the answer—someone to love is the answer.
Make someone happy, make just one person happy
and you will be happy too.
—Jimmy Durante, "Make Someone Happy"

I was flying down the freeway.

No, Jimmy, I wasn't a happy camper.

My wife was not making me happy. You had to be there.

Like a raving, Gumby-eyed lunatic at the controls of an intercontinental Concorde jet ready to snap the exploding whip of the sound barrier, I *VAAROOOOM-DAH*ed down the cow pasture–lined highway at over one hundred miles an hour. On the wrong side of the road. With the pink rental car speedometer tickling 107, nothing was moving faster than this Hertz hurricane of fury except my eyes, looking everywhere at once for Barney Fife to pull me over.

Clutching a pathetic, wrinkled rental car map, I precariously balanced the steering wheel in my left hand while attempting to read the microscopic words and squiggles directing me to the car rental return area. Blood surged through my veins as my anger spiked at the thought of a British map-maker laughing at silly, frantic Americans careening into smelly cow fields while trying to read the extra-fine print.

"Uuuggghhh," I screamed as I locked my leg onto the accelerator and launched a series of stammered outbursts audible only to the empty passenger seats. "WE'RE-GO-ING-TO-MIIISSSS-THEEE-PLA-AA-A-NE!"

Maybe I was temporarily going insane? Maybe I ate some bad British burger and had contracted the "Mad Cow" disease?

No way. This wasn't my fault.

My wife, Krista, and mother-in-law, Betty, were at the Heathrow International Airport terminal where I had dropped them off fifteen minutes earlier.

It was the end of our London vacation and I was doing my best Clark Griswold impersonation.

An hour earlier, I was told we were going to spend "just a few minutes" at the Laura Ashley shop in downtown London. Just real quick.

"You wait in the car," they told me.

Laura Ashley-Smashley-Mashley.

I waited. That was my first mistake.

"Just a few minutes" turned into an hour as Krista and Betty oohhed and aahed over floral prints, elegant sweeping dresses, mommy and me matching outfits, bedspreads, wallpaper, curtains, stationery sets, toilet roll holders, Prince Charles earwax removal kits . . . you get the picture.

Three times I sounded the five-minute warning.

Should've called James Bond.

A handsome 007 would have stolen their attention.

Should've called Henry VIII.

Didn't Anne Boleyn shop at Laura Ashley?

Now I was a lost Mario Andretti wannabe fumbling over fouled-up directions, doing God only knows how many kilometers per hour, while coaching myself in the fundamental driving techniques of the Motherland, "Stay to the *left* of the road. STAY LEFT. STAY LEFT."

The plane was leaving, not boarding, for America in fifteen minutes.

Bingo. Finally found the car return. Stormed inside and was warmly greeted by a cordial British car rental return manager who queried, "Might you be Mr. O'Connor? I just received a phone call from your wife who's wondering where you are."

Visualize rage.

After silently simmering on a shuttle bus slower than a late-afternoon English tea, I bounded off the bus and through the electronic doors at the main terminal. Standing next to an x-ray security station, Krista and Betty waved me down and yelled their only foreign words of the whole trip, "Hurry! We're going to miss the plane! What took you so long?"

Excuse me? Did I just hear what I just heard? What took ME so long?

Mother, daughter, and the fang-bearing American Werewolf in London son-in-law dashed through the first security station where polite British officers scanned our Laura Ashley bags and checked for terrorist bombs. I wouldn't be a bit surprised if one of Laura's clerks slipped a big boomer in the bag. Good ol' Laura certainly terrorized me all afternoon long. A few more scenarios like this and I'd be ready to get back to my Irish roots by joining the IRA.

We sprinted twenty paces only to be halted again by a second security station.

"Why are there so many x-ray machines?" Krista said out loud. "We're never going to make the plane!"

The snapping, popping, stinging spark of my anger finally detonated.

"Krista! This! Is! Not!! The! United! States! Of! America! We-are-in-a-foreign-country-where-bombs-explode-eh-ver-ree-hee-day!"

When the smoke finally cleared, my claws retracted and the three of us began running toward our gate through a marathon series of hallways. Our gate, #1,851, was the last gate, the farthest away from the curb, about as close as you can get to the border of the former Soviet Union.

Dressed in wool sweaters, thick overcoats, and long every-thing for the nip of English weather . . . plus, loaded down with—yes, you got it—Laura Ashley dresses, Laura Ashley kids' clothes, Laura Ashley power tools, sweat poured down our faces as we half-ran, half-speed-walked down the labyrinthine hallways of Heathrow International Airport.

In my mind, anger bubbled and popped in a thick, meaty stew. *Fine. This is just fine . . . I hope we miss the stupid flight. I don't care one bit. I hope, I hope, I hope we miss the plane.*

Bumbling along, I looked at the sweat-drenched faces of Krista and Betty. They both looked back at me and went bal-listic in sidesplitting laughter.

Reciting the polar opposite of what I was thinking, they launched another volley of laughter and screamed, "We can make it! C'mon . . . keep going! We can make it!"

Tears streamed down Krista's and Betty's faces as they cried all the louder at the sight of the tortured scowl on my mug. Open mockery.

Funny. Real funny. Laughter as a defense mechanism, right?

Finally, we arrived at our gate and were met by an airline attendant wildly waving her arms.

"Hurry, they're going to shut the airplane door," she cried.

Huffing, puffing, perspiring, almost expiring, we boarded the airplane. A flight attendant stopped us in the aisle and apologized, "I'm sorry, but your seats in Coach Class were taken. We had to bump all of you to First Class."

Krista's eyes lit up like landing lights and met my bloodshot, narrowed slits. Tilting her head to one side, she beamed in surprise. "See, isn't it a good thing we were late!"

Common Ground

The English Airport Story still gets a lot of laughs between Krista, Betty, and me. As Krista maintains, I was the one who got lost. I was the one who showed up at the airport last. "I wasn't late," she mocks. "We were waiting and waiting at the airport for you!"

Guys, you know how this one goes, get on my side here.

"No, no, no . . . I came into the Laura Ashley shop three times—*uno, dos, tres*—and said we were late for the plane. But no, you two had to shop and shop and shop. If we had arrived at the airport on time, I would have had plenty of time to get lost and still make it to the terminal on time. How was I supposed to know I needed an electron microscope to read that terrible map?"

"It doesn't matter," Krista holds firm. "You were still late."

Krista and I know now that Laura Ashley, rental cars, and international travel are as dangerous for our marriage as driving on the wrong side of the road. Yes, flying in first class for ten hours was slick, but the events leading up to first class bordered on marital hijacking.

It is so easy to go to extremes. I don't know about you, but somewhere between the wedding altar, having a couple of kids, struggling with finances, learning how to be a selective listener, changing jobs, coping with chronic illness, dealing with in-laws, moving (circle 1, 3, 5, 10 times), figuring out what letter of s-e-x contains the secret of complete and total fulfillment, mundane chores, death, and taxes, it's not too hard for couples to go to extremes.

Marriage is an extreme state. What other institution besides a mental institution brings completely different, somewhat crazy people together for a long time and expects them to get along?

Women are always right and men are never wrong for a lot of very strong reasons, many of which we'll explore in this book, but you'd better be ready to laugh because I'm coming out with both guns blazing. I know darn well that it will be mostly wives who pick up this book and buy it first. So if you're a guy and your wife has gone to the extreme of putting you under house arrest until you read this book, understand that I've written this book with you, the husband/prisoner, in mind. It is a guy-friendly book, and I am taking no prisoners, husbands or wives.

All of us have gone to extremes and deserve to be teased for what we put our poor spouses through in the name of love and commitment. Laughing at this is a serious requirement for a healthy marriage. This book will help you and your spouse avoid going to extremes by showing you how to find and get on common ground in your marriage. Common ground is that essential place in every marriage where husbands and wives understand each other's needs and wants by sharing mutual interests, values, beliefs, dreams, goals, and desires. Extremes are what knock couples off of common ground, which leads to resentment, distance, and hurt feelings in the marriage.

Married couples who find and stay on common ground experience deeper intimacy, greater satisfaction, and longer happiness in marriage than anyone else. Why? Because by accepting, respecting, and supporting each other, these couples can discuss differences, share dreams, value personality differences, tolerate quirks, and tell disgusting habits to leave the room.

Going to extremes is a very real part of married life. Why? Because of the simple truth men don't want to admit that women are always right, and likewise because women don't understand that men are never wrong. In the next few chapters you'll discover the secrets of why women are always right and men are never wrong, but more important, you'll discover some practical and positive ways to find and build on the common ground in your marriage without going to extremes. This book will help you pay attention so that you may better understand and laugh at the unique way your spouse is wired. In every chapter, you will find a "Common Ground" section that will give you solid and helpful tools for creating a healthy, more loving marriage.

But be forewarned: If you laugh, you just may learn something.

Aren't You Being a Little Extreme?

2

My wife's jealousy is getting ridiculous. The other day she looked at my calendar and demanded to know who May was.
—Rodney Dangerfield

If you want to know the real reason why women are always right and men are never wrong, you have to look no further than the new breed of extreme sports. Millions of American men and women have grown tired of scaling Mt. Everest, running in marathons and triathlons, jungle trekking in Borneo, and outrunning polar bears every year in the Alaskan Iditarod race. Men and women across the nation are forgoing rock climbing, skysurfing, bungee jumping, and yes, even the prestigious Raid Gauloise, for a higher level of adrenaline-inducing athletic endurance and new levels of heightened awareness. Like never before, men and women are rising to the challenge of pushing the extreme envelope in bold and challenging ways. Only the few, the brave, the truly inspirational, live on the edge of these new, death-defying extreme sports—

Marathon Bathroom Reading. For a man, scaling every peak in the Rocky Mountain range is child's play compared to scaling the Great White Throne for hour upon hour of mental stimulation. Classified ads, junk mail, *War and Peace, Good Housekeeping, Curious George Goes to the Hospital, Elimination for Dummies*—it doesn't matter what the printed material is, if a man has to go, he's got to read something on the potty. Anything.

If your husband is a bona fide member of the Bathroom Book of the Month Club, you've undoubtedly wondered how it is that the man you married can live for three minutes without air, three days without water, and three months without food, but can't live for three seconds without having something to read on the john. This extreme sport, which millions of men are flocking to, is bound to please the shareholders of Procter & Gamble.

Martha Stewart Anything. This lady has developed a cult following of female fanatics willing to do anything to learn how to cut a perfect slice of celery.

Martha slices. She dices. She chops and purées. She has made Ronco's Vegamatic obsolete.

She is a marketing revolutionary with her own TV and radio show, web site, magazine, lube and oil change franchise, cooking boot camps, skywriting recipe service, camouflage shower curtains, and the master key to your wife's heart. That includes your ATM PIN number. Martha Stewart has given Julia Child the boot and is single-handedly responsible for the extreme sport of colonizing, accessorizing, kitchenizing, cookerizing, remodelizing, and spendisizing every available cent in the modern American home. Look out for the limited edition collector's set of Martha Stewart Ginsu Knives. You'll weep when you see how easily the celery slices.

Satellite Channel Surfing. Hey dude, drop into your imitation Naugahyde La-Z-Boy and this extreme sport'll launch you into the stratosphere as you simultaneously watch the entire NCAA National Basketball championship series, golf cart etiquette tips on the Golf Channel, widemouth bass fishing on the Go Fish Channel (Hey Martha! Look at da size uh dose gills!), and the 19th Annual Trailerpark Pull. Though extreme male adherents to couchpotatodom have remarkable dexterity skills to handle four remotes at once, many extreme channel surfers do experience a hazardous, painful, burning condition in their right thumb commonly known as "remotitis." That affliction, along with weight gain, social isolation (see "Marathon Bathroom Reading"), junk food indigestion, recliner repair bills, and whatever injury a frustrated wife sustains when the alleged male channel surfer refuses to surrender the remote are just a few of the dangers faced by those who ride the wild waves of five hundred-plus channels. Cowabunga!

Other extreme sports that are gaining momentum for men and ready to explode to the forefront of this new craze are Picking and Scratching (an ESPN X-Games version of Jane Goodall's work with chimpanzees); Map Reading 101; and Lost Keys, Wallet, and Watch Exploration.

For women, the newest extreme sports include Carpool Crosstraining (the amazing ability to drive a carload of screaming kids, balance the family checkbook, apply makeup, listen to Dr. Laura, and sip a skinny, dressed decaf Mocha Grande from Starbucks at forty miles an hour), All-Girl-All-Night-Bunko-Gambling-Parties-While-Husband-Struggles-at-Home-to-Get-the-Kids-to-Bed-before-11:00-P.M., and the risky female venture of Bathroom Soloing.

What do these extreme sports tell us about men and women? Men and women are born competitors—*that's the real reason why women are always right and men are never wrong.* Women don't want to be dominated by men, and men don't want to be dominated by women. Men and women go to extremes when they feel the other person is trying to get the upper, controlling hand in the relationship. Both sides want to be right and nobody wants to be wrong. Unfortunately, this truth is discovered by most couples not *before* they get married, but *after.* Let me explain—

Before marriage, men compete against men and women compete against women to see who gets who for life. A guy competes to get his girl, and a woman competes to get her ring. When a man finally gets over his fear of commitment, which ranks right up there with the fear of household chores, nasty French poodles, and really big, expensive diamond rings, he humbles himself for a brief moment and asks for her hand in marriage. At this rare, vulnerable moment, the poor schlep is ready to crawl into the sewer system for life if she says no.

The woman, who at this instant has more power than any world leader, relishes watching this desperate dog of a man hide behind pathetic, imploring puppy eyes. She doesn't make him suffer too long. She realizes that she also had to compete, scratch, and pull the hair of other women to get Mr. Right to notice her and thus bring him to his knees. She, too, professes her love and promises her troth. Whatever that is.

Now, after Mr. and Mrs. Right seal their wedding vows with a big, wet, juicy kiss, the competition does not stop. The newly married dynamic duo soon become the dueling duo. They no longer compete against marauding predators trying to steal their quarry; instead, they now compete against one other.

Reality hits within the first few years of marriage. Dishes are left in the sink for days. Toilet paper is not properly placed on the roller. (We'll get to that one later!) Clothes are left on the floor. Morning breath supplants the need for hair curlers.

Accounting techniques for checkbook balances are challenged. Words, gestures, and facial expressions of in-laws are duly misinterpreted. Foreplay becomes as unpredictable as the weather. Credit card expenditures are questioned. Tax deductions are born and cared for. Subtle hints and expectations of flowers, love notes, and phone calls from work fall on deaf and really dumb ears. Dinner becomes a sumptuous choice between Corn Flakes, Lucky Charms, or 100% All Bran cereal.

Mrs. Right is now Mrs. Wrong.

Mr. Right is now Mr. Big Jerkhead.

Both sides go to extremes in competing against one another . . . why else do they call it the "battle of the sexes"? Somewhere in between, there is common ground and that is the basis for serving one another in love.

Common Ground

Before you were married, you had to compete for the love and attention of your romantic pursuit. Now that you're married, you're still competing for that same love and attention. When you don't get what you want in marriage, you have to compete for it. Husbands and wives often want more from one another than they want to give. It's in our competitive and comparative nature to want our own way.

Women don't want to be kept down and men don't want to be put down. When you compete against your spouse, you are competing for the things you want and need as a person. You're competing for what every married person wants and needs: love, attention, respect, admiration, listening, provision, understanding, intimacy, leadership, approval, sex, time, companionship, and friendship. If you've ever said to your spouse, "Honey, aren't you being a little too extreme?" understand that he or she is going to extremes because of some felt want or need for something from you.

If your spouse is a workaholic, you're not competing against the firm. If you and your spouse are having schedule conflicts, you're not competing against time. If you and your spouse never get any time alone because of the kids, you're not competing against the kids. If you and your spouse get in arguments over finances, you're not competing against money. If you and your spouse fight about in-laws, you're not competing against your in-laws. Guess who your number one competitor is? You got it—the person who slid that ring on your finger and promised to meet your every want and need. As much as humanly possible, that is. You were married in the eyes of God, not to God.

In one way or another, all spouses compete against each other and every couple has their own strategies to get what they want from each other. This may be a shocking revelation for some of you who are thinking, *Compete against my spouse? We don't compete or argue—we love one another.* That's just like my father's clients. He's a funeral director and his clients never argue about how they're treated either.

As fun as it is to joke about the extreme differences between husbands and wives, I don't know anyone who likes living with a spouse who goes to extremes. We're all guilty of going to extremes. We all do it. Every husband and wife goes to extremes, but after a while, living in an extreme state—a marriage characterized by extremes—gets old and weary. Extremes quickly take the fun and joy out of being married. Marriage is not designed to be characterized by extremes. That "two" are supposed to be "one" is premarital counseling 1A, but extremes divide a marriage by getting couples off the common ground that keeps their marriage healthy, alive, and enjoyable.

What makes a marriage work is not competition, but cooperation. Look at the word: *co-operate*. That means working together. Each side fully invested to make the marriage a success. If one person isn't fully invested in the marriage, you can count on the marriage going to unhealthy extremes. What does it take to cooperate in a marriage? What does it take to get on common ground?

In a word, grace.

If you want to work on having a great marriage, the one extreme to lean on is grace. Your husband needs grace. Your wife needs grace. Grace is the gift you give your spouse with no requirement to earn your time, love, or attention. (Even when it's not deserved.) Grace is the common ground that can make a marriage grow. Grace happens when a husband and wife offer each other the freedom to grow and learn at a comfortable time and pace. Not yours. If you give your spouse grace by not singling out faults and character flaws, but instead decide to work on the kinks in your own character, what you're doing is making your relationship a safe environment for growth and change. That sends your spouse the clear signal that you're willing to cooperate in order to make your marriage work.

Giving your spouse grace doesn't mean letting him or her be an out-of-control eighteen-wheeler and you're desert road kill. Giving grace sometimes means telling the truth in a way that may wound, but doesn't kill. It often begins with telling your spouse the truth of how you feel about your marriage and then cooperating with your spouse to make the changes your marriage needs. Too many marriages stay stuck in extremes because one or both spouses have stopped extending grace to the other spouse. Grace enables you and your spouse to be safe in each other's presence.

When you and your spouse are not in an extreme state, ask each other, "When do we go to extremes? What are the major sources of irritation that make us really bug one another? If there were one or two issues that would sink our marriage, what would they be? How can we stop competing against each other and begin cooperating so we can manage our marriage truly well?"

When you and your spouse go to extremes, regardless of who's right or wrong, it takes cooperation and grace to get your marriage back on common ground. Cooperation is the common ground that makes your marriage work. Grace is what'll get you there.

I'm Right and You're Wrong

3

*Marriage is when a man and woman become as one;
the trouble starts when they try to decide which one.*

i can remember getting home from school when I was a kid, raiding the refrigerator, and lying down on our lime-green shag carpet to watch one of my favorite television shows, *Get Smart*. I loved laughing at the Chief, Larabee, Hymie the CONTROL robot, Siegfried, Schtarker, Admiral Hargrade, and, of course, the ever self-confident, but completely clumsy Secret Agent Maxwell Smart. I also had a crush on Agent 99, but what guy didn't? I always wished we had a telephone booth with a secret elevator in our house. What I really needed was the "Cone of Silence" so my parents couldn't hear my friends and me sharing our fifth-grade secrets. Never could find a pair of those telephone shoes.

Whenever Maxwell Smart was surrounded by KAOS agents or hanging upside down over a pool of hungry alligators, what did he always do to get out of his predicament? He went to extremes. In his sharp, shrill voice, Maxwell Smart resorted to blustery warnings of cataclysmic harm if anyone laid a finger on him. Who could forget such classic Maxwell Smart lines as these:

- At this very minute, twenty-five CONTROL agents are converging on this building. Would you believe two squad cars and a motorcycle cop? How about a vicious street cleaner and a toothless police dog?

- As soon as you're gone, by the use of sheer brute strength I shall be able to rip these chains from the wall in one minute. Would you believe it? One minute. Would you believe two minutes? How about a week from Tuesday?

- You better drop that gun because this yacht happens to be surrounded by the Seventh Fleet. Would you believe the Sixth Fleet? How about a school of angry flounder?

- In a short while, General Crawford and a hundred of his crack paratroopers will come crashing into this landing. Would you believe J. Edgar Hoover and ten of his G-men? How about Tarzan and a couple of apes? Bomba the Jungle Boy?

Because Maxwell Smart was desperate to escape the evil clutches of KAOS agents, he naturally went to extremes. Daily, he and Agent 99 battled KAOS agents who were pursuing world domination. Though Max was a CONTROL agent, we all know that his life and the perplexing pickles he found himself in were anything but controlled. He had to single-hand-

edly outwit KAOS agents who tried to outsmart him with dastardly deeds like:

- The old bulletproof-cummerbund-in-the-tuxedo trick.

- The old remote-control-self-propelled-spinning-door-
  knob trick.

- The old drug-his-prunes, fake-the-fight, ransack-the-
  apartment, and switch-places-with-the-Admiral trick.

- The old Professor-Peter-Peckinpah-all-purpose-anti-
  personnel-pocket-pistol-under-the-toupee trick.

When you and your spouse square off and say to each other
in one way or another, "I'm right and you're wrong," what
you've got going on is a battle between KAOS and CON-
TROL. It's the old you-won't-win-this-one-no-matter-how-
hard-you-pout-scream-whine-huff-slam-the-door-I'm-not-sleep-
ing-on-the-couch-*YOU-SLEEP-ON-THE-COUCH*-what-in-
the-world-was-I-thinking-when-I-married-you-somebody-
must've-slipped-me-a-mickey trick. Each spouse is claiming
that they're on the CONTROL team.

I'm Maxwell Smart.

No, I'm Agent 99.

Nobody wants to be the bad guy.

Nobody wants to be Siegfried, the leader of KAOS.

One of the first things Krista and I learned in our premarital counseling class was that we were to remove two extreme
words from our soon-to-be marriage vocabulary: *always* and
never. We were clearly told never to say "always" and never to
say "never."

Ever.

What was that counselor smoking? *Always* and *never* are the twin silver bullets of every good argument. *Always* and *never* are the North and South Poles for every point, principle, or position on the compass of marital communication. They are the moral high ground for winning your way in marriage. There is no more effective way to put your spouse on the defensive than staking your claim on either side of *always* and *never*. What better way to make your point than by using such precise, authoritative, righteous, and wieldy-sounding words: *You always do this—you never do that.*

Always is the best offense and *never* is the best defense.

Always and *never* are the Malta of the Marriage Mediterranean.

Control these two words and you control the world!

Now I know you and your spouse would never, never, never, ever think of going to extremes by using these two nasty words. Right? It doesn't matter if you've been married for three minutes or thirty years, you *do know* the drill for using the extremes of *always* and *never*—

- You *never* call when you're going to be late. *Check the phone bill. I always call.*

- You *never* give me any help with the kids. *I am like their personal au pair!*

- You *never* want to have sex. *We did last month!*

- You *always* side with your parents when we're with them. *I never do . . . I think for myself.*

- You *never* do anything around here. *Me? I do everything around here.*

- You *always* pay more attention to the kids than me! *Okay, let's make love.*

- You're *always* nagging me! *I don't nag . . . you have the memory of a newt.*

- You *never* talk to me. *I always speak when spoken to.*

- You're *always* more interested in ESPN than me. *That's not fair.*

- You *never* let me go out with the guys. *You're married to your friends!*

- You're *always* late. *I'm never late getting my hair done.*

- You *never* pay the bills on time. *I pay the bills like clockwork.*

- You know_____ and _____ *never* talk to each other this way. (Fill in the name of the Ken and Barbie couple you know who can do no wrong. Now go toilet-paper their house and spray shaving cream all over her pink Corvette.)

Common sense tells us that women aren't always right and men are sometimes wrong, but what does common sense have to do with marriage? Some of the best arguments in marriage make absolutely no sense at all.

But when you are in a fight with your husband, it doesn't matter what he says: You're right and you know it. *Women are always, always right.*

When you're in a fight with your wife, it doesn't matter what she says: You're never wrong and you know it. *Men are never, ever wrong.*

Which is why both of you are always right and never wrong, right?

Wrong.

Common Ground

Scientists have confirmed that marriage is the most extreme relationship among all living things. Except perhaps for the black widow and her soon-to-be-eaten mate, marriage is the epitome of extremes in God's wild kingdom. Put a man and woman together for a few years, throw in a couple of kids, some pets, a mortgage, conflicting schedules, job stress, a stack of bills thicker than the wad in your wallet, and the natural order is chaos. Marriage is anything but control.

As a CONTROL agent, Maxwell Smart understood this important scientific principle, and so he threw caution to the wind and flew by the seat of his pants. In the midst of chaos, he was unflappable. Unstoppable. Brazenly bold. Supremely confident. And why?

Max knew he couldn't control all the chaos, but the one thing he could control was himself.

Maybe Max and Agent 99 have something to teach us all about marriage. Life is a constant, changing state of chaos and control. And marriage may be an accurate reflection of this broken world that causes aliens looking at us from outer space to scratch their antennae and wonder, "What on earth are these people doing?"

The illusion of control we strive for in marriage is as elusive as getting help from an HMO customer service representative. There is never one part of any marriage that is completely under control. Just when you think you've got your finances under control, the transmission goes out on your car. Just when you think you've raised the perfect kid, the vice principal is on the phone. Just when you think you're a romantic Don Juan, your wife calls you Señor Postmortem.

The heart of most spousal skirmishes is the need to be in control. When one spouse feels threatened by the other, it's easy to go to extremes. When no one wants to back down and admit when they're truly wrong, then what you have is chaos.

As humans, we hate to admit when we're wrong. We attempt to control the situation, problem, or conflict by wanting to be right and never admitting we're wrong. We may even be willing to put up with high degrees of chaos until the other person backs down or caves in first. We don't like looking at the chaos in our own hearts. It's far easier to take inventory of our spouse's character flaws and mistakes than to do a personal inventory of our own. Instead of taking control of our own actions and attitudes, it's so much easier to try to control our spouse. It's far preferable to be right than to be wrong. Wrong is an admission of failure, and that is about as un-American as driving a Honda in Detroit.

Getting on common ground is work, and building a marriage that is constantly changing amid the chaos of life is hard work. It means being willing to look at problems, conflicts, and situations from our spouse's perspective. It means giving up our need for control. It means admitting that there is more chaos in our life than we'd like to admit, that we don't have it all together. It means admitting that we're not always very smart.

If you and your husband or wife want to get smart, you won't try to control each other. If you try to control your spouse, get ready for chaos. Give up control and look where you need to change rather than trying to change your spouse. Instead of controlling your spouse, do the hard work of teaming with him or her by getting on common ground. That means getting on common ground with how you speak and communicate with each other. It means getting on common ground with how you respect, help, and treat each other. It means getting on common ground with how you raise your kids. It means getting on common ground with how you express your love, intimacy, and sexuality. It means getting on common ground regarding your faith, your finances, your time, your friendships, your values and beliefs.

Ultimately, in the larger scheme of things, it doesn't matter who's right and who's wrong—if you're really in your marriage for the long haul the way you promised, the only way and the best way to move forward is by getting on common ground.

If you've recently gone to extremes with your spouse and pulled a marital red card, go ahead and wave the white flag. Say you're sorry. Forgive as God has forgiven you. Ask God for peace in the midst of the chaos. Get on common ground. Talk about your differences and celebrate the fact that your spouse is not your clone. If that were the case, you'd really have chaos.

Appreciate the unique differences in your spouse instead of allowing those differences to divide you. Control yourself, not your spouse. Do this and you'll get smart.

Mr. Fix-It &
Mrs. Feel-It
4

I do nothing that a man of unlimited funds, superb physical
endurance, and maximum scientific knowledge could not do.
—Batman

In maledom, there are guys who can make, build, or fix anything. These guys are *Men* with a capital *M*. And then, there
are guys like me who get lost driving to Home Depot, who
can't tell the difference between a wing nut and a walnut, and
whose wives refuse to allow them to use power tools out of fear
of turning the garage into a body parts shop. These are normal
guys, also called *Losers* with a capital *L*.

Like great white sharks, the guys who can build a redwood
deck in forty-five minutes or dismantle a semitruck blindfolded
or drill for oil in their backyards, are Manly Men who swim at
the top of the home improvement food chain.

Normal guys like me hang out at the lower rungs of the
food chain, somewhere between single-cell protozoa and mold
spores. When I was running around as a kid wearing my six-
gun cowboy holster and shooting up the neighborhood, those

other guys were wearing their dads' tool belts and building tree houses that are still standing today. Yeah, now they may be able to build anything with their bare hands, but I'm still a crack shot with my cap gun.

Asking me to install, let's say, a sprinkler system is equivalent to asking me to perform brain surgery. My only two marketable home improvement skills are painting and gardening. There's nothing I can't fix with a gallon of spackle. If I'm out of nails, I'll hang pictures with spackle. If the garbage disposal is busted, I'll spackle it. If the roof has a four-foot hole in it, I'll spackle it.

There's nothing in our home that can't be fixed with spackle. Especially when my wife goes away for the weekend. I'm terrible at brushing my girls' hair and making ponytails. So I just spackle 'em. Only have to do their hair once and it's good for the whole weekend.

Not only am I Mr. Spackle, I can also mow. *I'm an excellent lawn mower.* There was a time, however, I didn't see our neighbor's poodle dart in front of the oncoming lawn mower blades. Except for a rare lawn kill, I can usually mow my entire lawn without taking out any sprinkler heads. (Poodles do make a good turf builder—lots of nitrogen.)

Unlike yours truly, Manly Men can do just about anything. These guys are also known as Mr. Fix-Its and my buddy Glen is one of them. Glen is one of those Swiss Family Robinson–type guys: If he ever gets lost in the woods with a butter knife and a roll of kite string, he'll build an entire shopping mall in a month. He has more tools in his garage than McDonnell Douglas and Boeing combined. Glen is so amazing I am tempted to worship at his feet. *But I am not woorrrthy!*

The other day I went over to his house to help him work on a new fence he was building. On previous weekends, Glen had surveyed, dug, poured, and built the cinder-block wall that served as the foundation for the fence, which just happened to circumscribe his entire house. Then, he did something called "tonguing and grooving" with five-foot sections of cedar board and connected them to perfectly spaced steel poles cemented into the cinder blocks.

It's a well-known labor principle that work always goes faster with two people. That is, two people who know what they're doing. In our case, there was Glen, who knew exactly what he was doing. And me, who was clueless. That meant Glen now had one and one-sixteenth persons working on his fence.

Glen wouldn't let me touch his table saw, which I thought looked real neat. I'd never been that close to a table saw before. The way it was designed, though, didn't make that much sense to me. How was a guy supposed to cut wood with a sharp, round blade? At least a regular saw had a handle on it. When Glen put a stack of cedar onto the table saw, I smirked and thought to myself, *This'll be interesting.*

Then he flipped the switch.

That dang thing screamed to life like an F-16 bomber doing a flyby.

He scared the living daylights outta me; nearly had a heart attack.

Got that itchy sawdust down my shirt too.

Now I know why they call those things power tools.

Women don't share the same inferiority complex I have about fixing things primarily because women aren't concerned with fixing things.

Women like to fix people. This is because women are feelers. This isn't a bad thing because without women, this world would be a much colder, less loving, less compassionate planet.

But for some women who are strong *feelers* and get emotionally involved in the affairs of other people, what they *feel* can get them into trouble. Here we see the close relationship between feelings and power tools.

When there is a problem, regardless of skill or know-how, a man will dive right in and try to fix it. A woman, however, first needs to figure out how she *feels* about the problem before deciding on the proper methodology to fix it, which then requires a whole different set of feelings.

And how does a woman figure out how she feels but by talking to other women?

This is where the trouble usually begins.

Let's say a woman feels really discouraged about constantly arguing with her teenage daughter. At this point, she isn't looking for answers or solutions. *She's just feeling.* She's tried just about everything and the only thing she needs is someone to listen to her feelings.

So she meets another mom for coffee and pours her heart out over expensive café mochas, which account for one-eighth of the family's annual budget. As she explains how her daughter talks back, ignores curfew, and runs with a creepy crowd of kids, the other mom's heart goes out to her as she listens attentively. This mom *feels* her friend's pain because she, too, experienced the same struggles a year earlier with her own teenage daughter, who's now serving a life sentence in prison.

The listening mom can't help but get teary-eyed as she hears her friend's lament. The woman with the wayward daughter is beginning to feel better because her friend is listening and she's finally able to understand why she feels the way she feels.

After a moment of brief silence between the two, the listening mom is now emotionally invested in her friend's problem and feels obligated to help her fix it, so she starts in with the best advice she feels she can offer.

"Have you tried tough love? Have you sat down and told your daughter straight up that you're not going to take any more lip from her? Have you suspended privileges, taken away her TV and phone time? Have you called the parents of the friends she's running with? Have you bought a drug testing kit? A retina scanner? Have you gotten Glen to build you a twelve-foot barbed-wire fence around your house? *I did all these things, and you wouldn't believe the change I saw in my daughter!*"

The discouraged mom is taken aback. She was just beginning to feel better. She thought she'd finally found someone who could relate to what she was going through. All she'd wanted was someone to connect with, someone to listen to her. And now, here was this mother-of-a-convict implying that she didn't know how to parent.

She must think I'm a really bad mother. She must think I don't know a thing about raising kids. She probably thinks my daughter's real problem is me—what NERVE!

Common Ground

One of the most significant reasons men and women go to extremes is because of the different ways they are wired.

Men are fixers and women are feelers. Don't misunderstand me, though; women are fixers too. They just approach problems differently from men. In general, guys lean toward the logical, rational way of looking at problems, and women lean toward what their heart is telling them about the problem.

Understanding this basic difference between men and women will help you better understand your spouse. Too many arguments in marriage are based on the silent, unspoken premise that men should know what their wives are feeling and women should logically know and do what their husbands are thinking.

Whenever there is a problem or conflict in marriage, men prefer to fix the problem right away so they can get back to whatever they were doing. Women, on the other hand, also want to resolve the problem, but in order to get to a resolution, they need to map the emotional landscape of the problem to make sure no feeling about the problem has been left unturned. Sometimes a woman doesn't always know what she's feeling, and the first step to solving the problem is figuring out her feelings. Fixing the problem isn't so immediate a priority to her as making sure her husband understands and accepts how she feels about the problem.

Both people, if they're committed to working out the conflict, will want to work toward resolution, but how they get there will often involve two completely different routes.

So what are helpful things to remember when you and your spouse go to extremes and you're mutually trying to resolve a conflict? Is it possible to get on common ground when men and women are wired so differently?

Guys, instead of trying to do an immediate spackle job on the problem, first listen to your wife's feelings about her perception of what has happened. Listening to your wife will help her get to the root of what she's feeling. When some women are upset, all they can see is a whole bunch of jumbled feelings. It helps a woman to talk those feelings out in order to get clarity about the most important things she's feeling. By being patient and attentive to what she has to say, you are actually working toward a quicker resolution. So, try not to give immediate advice or solve the problem for her. This will only frustrate her by making her feel you're not listening.

Wives, what a guy thinks is often more important to him than what he feels. Guys like to think that their ideas and opinions matter to their wives. When the problem can't be immediately solved or when it's stymied because you're not sure of what you're feeling about the problem, this is frustrating to Mr. Fix-It. Now that he's frustrated, the next emotion your husband is most in touch with is anger. This is the same emotion that hurts your feelings because you don't like your husband to be angry, even though your husband may not necessarily be angry at you. He's angry because he's frustrated at the unresolved conflict he thinks he can fix!

Like you, your husband has the need to get the problem resolved, but his way of getting there will be different from yours. He cannot read your mind and know what you're feeling unless you tell him what you're feeling. Though you may not like him giving you ideas about how to solve the conflict, that's the logical side of him speaking and it's his way of being helpful.

Both you and your spouse can best serve each other by asking each other specific questions designed to help you better understand one another: "What are your feelings about this problem? From your perspective, what do you think are the major issues involved? What do you think or feel is the best way to resolve this problem? What options do you suggest we consider? Have I said or done anything that has hurt you?"

Now listen to each other. *Really listen.*

By sharing patience, consideration, and forgiveness and exploring the options you both develop, you can land on common ground to solve the problem even though you're wired far differently. Fixing and feeling are important facets of every marriage, and neither quality is exclusive to a specific sex. By recognizing the predominant way our spouses are wired, we're better able to accept them for who they are.

The next time you and your spouse are going to extremes, take a time-out and ask each other these questions. Perhaps you'll get to a quicker resolution, and you won't need any spackle.

Not Another One of Those Parties!

5

Maybe you've heard about the man whose credit card
was stolen, but decided not to report it.
The thief was spending less than his wife.

If your wife likes clothes, beauty products, personal security devices, cookware, photo albums, long-distance communications, decorative stamp pads, vitamins, children's toys, and just about any product available on the face of this earth, chances are you married a party animal.

If your wife isn't a party animal yet, you're either recently married or recently lobotomized. In the latter case, I can't do anything to help you, except perhaps lend you my jigsaw for any corrective surgery you want to perform on yourself. In the former case, I have a warning: Just you wait.

A recent discussion with my buddies confirms that all of our wives are party animals and that there is a racket going on in corporate America for housewives looking to earn a few extra dollars a week so they can "retire" in less than a year. It goes something like this—

Every few months or so, our wives get invited to attend "a party," hosted by a friend of a friend who is going to get a lot of "free" merchandise for hosting "the party." This enterprising hostess has invited everybody (*a*) whom she remotely knows, (*b*) who owes her a favor, and (*c*) who, like her, has no money.

Before I further extrapolate upon this unique cultural phenomenon, a brief explanation of previously mentioned terms is required. These all-fcmale outings are not parties—they are department stores in motion. They are in-home sales meetings designed to sell you product, product, and, when you run out, more product.

Especially you soon-to-be-married or young married guys, did you get the gist of that last line? Read my lips: C-O-N-T-I-N-U-A-L F-I-N-A-N-C-I-A-L D-R-A-I-N!

Don't be hoodwinked. A party, as most people understand it, is a celebration for an important event such as a birthday, holiday, or special occasion like the Super Bowl. Buying or selling the latest gizmowhatchamacallit, cheese slicer, greaseless facial cream, toy puzzle, or chelated B vitamin does not justify calling these sales spiels "parties." To do so violates the traditional definition of the word. However, women will bend the traditional definition of this word to elevate the importance of the event and thus secure their exit from the house for the evening.

Next, the word *free* is very misleading. I do admit that I have allowed a certain number of these "parties" in our home. (Two. No more.) All on the premise that my wife would receive "free" merchandise based upon how much product was sold to everyone who couldn't afford it in the first place.

By the time my wife bought and mailed the party invitations, hired a professional house cleaner, and shopped for the party essentials of flowers, hors d'oeuvres, food, drinks, and dessert, we were in the hole to the tune of two hundred big ones.

For three weeks of addressing, mailing, shopping, cleaning, phoning, and getting me and the kids out of the house for the night, she received a "free" pizza dish valued at thirty-five dollars.

I'm still working at Taco Bell on the weekends to pay off that one.

Now, guys, don't be fooled. Your wife will say this is an important party she must attend. The person selling the product will have an important, corporate-sounding title like "Independent Sales Representative," "Personal Wardrobe Consultant," "Itchin' to Cook in da' Kitchen Connoisseur," "Global Dream Team Disco Machine," or "CEO of P.O. Box 591."

At the "party," your wife and the other poor women in attendance will learn dozens of personal enrichment exercises for slicing onions into perfect trapezoids, strategically placing pictures in photo albums, warding off would-be attackers with lemon-scented pepper spray, applying enough facial cream to grease a cement truck, and swallowing enough antioxidant vitamins to rid the entire Los Angeles basin of smog.

Even if your wife isn't especially interested in buying anything, like all the other women there, she will feel insufferably *sorry* for the priestess pitching the product at preposterous prices. Yes, your wife will feel *guilty* if she buys nothing. Not only will she feel guilty, she will also feel *embarrassed* if she walks out the front door empty-handed. And why not?

The hostess is counting on her. Her "free" booty is based upon total sales.

The sales lady is counting on her. Her entire financial future is at stake.

Your wife's friends are counting on her. There is strength in numbers, and when each wife tells her husband that "everybody" was buying, your wife can't stand the idea of being the lone fasting shark in this financial feeding frenzy.

And so, your wife will give in to guilt and put you in the poorhouse.

All my buddies and I agree that, if our wives could have demonstrated a little financial control at these parties, by now we could have paid in cash for the trips to Europe, cruises in the Bahamas, and lazy days on the sun-soaked beaches of Hawaii they all dream about. Can we help it if they've traded sparkling diamonds for laundry soap and deodorant?

If there is ever a fire in his house, my buddy Scott says the first thing he's grabbing is his wife's creatively designed photo album. He's got more money invested in that thing than anything else in the house. The only reason my other buddy Glen keeps his wife's vitamin business going is so he can file a Schedule C loss on their tax return. To top it off, my other buddy Brad is determined to print his own catalog to unload the thousand dollars of inventory his wife purchased to start her own decorative stamping business.

Sorry, Brad. We ain't buying.

With all this haranguing about in-home sales meetings, you must think I'm a real party pooper. I'm not. Honest. If your wife is going to a lingerie party, give her the checkbook and VISA card, take a second on the house, borrow from your kid's college savings—anything. With this important purchase, you can both throw your own little get-together and really become party animals.

Common Ground

Now that I have bagged on all those little parties our wives attend, I have a little confession to make. A few years ago, I sold long-distance communication services to my family and friends for about six months. My job at the church where I worked was about to be eliminated. I was finishing grad school. My wife was due to give birth to our second child in a couple of months. I was desperate and I was scared.

Then came "The Opportunity."

As an Independent Representative of one of the fastest growing telecommunication companies in the whole universe, I now had my own business. I was "on the ground floor" of the multibillion-dollar telecommunications industry. Not only was I going to become a multimillionaire within two years' time, I was also going to save my family and friends "thousands of dollars" on their $18.62 long-distance phone bills.

I had a vision for my future.

I was going to "retire" about thirty years early.

I had meaning.

I had purpose.

I had significance.

I had 5 cents a minute from coast to coast.

There comes a time in almost every marriage when the common ground of job security suddenly shifts. A change in career for husband or wife, layoffs, firings, a downturn in the marketplace, or a failed business venture. All of these professional and financial factors create intense pressure in marriage and contribute to couples getting off common ground.

In our case, Krista and I shared the common ground of stability and security in a job I loved and depended on. Our common ground shifted with the loss of that job and a sudden need to acquire a new source of income. What I, my wife, and my family really needed at that time was a steady job and not an "opportunity" pitch. What I lacked in maturity and common sense, I made up for in enthusiastic self-employment zeal for selling a product I knew very little about.

When Krista expressed skepticism and doubt about my

new "business," I became defensive and said she was being unsupportive. We were clearly not on common ground, but I wouldn't hear a word about it. Fortunately, a number of freelance writing projects kept us from becoming financial road kill, but not without our share of disagreements over me becoming the next Bill Gates of telecommunications.

Yeah, I poke fun at all those parties, but there is a large number of legitimate business opportunities out there. Many home-based businesses provide families the chance for one spouse to earn needed additional income while still being able to raise the children.

Whatever you and your spouse decide to do, make sure the choice is right for both of you. Do your homework first. Get an accurate assessment of everything involved in this new business opportunity. How much money will you have to invest? How much time is required? How long will it take to show a profit? What risks are involved? What impact will this decision have on your whole family? What kind of advice do your closest family members and friends have to offer?

These are important questions for all couples to ask before jumping into any business opportunity. Asking these types of questions will help you and your spouse determine if you're on common ground or not. *Don't trade one set of financial and career problems for another set of problems.*

Whether you've got a great entrepreneurial idea to create a power washer strong enough to remove that nagging soap scum off shower doors, or if you're thinking about becoming a two-income family, or if you've been suddenly laid off, or if your spouse comes home from one of those parties with a great business opportunity, before you make any decision, make sure you are both on common ground regarding this issue. With any new opportunity, there are risks and rewards. Just make sure you and your spouse aren't going to extremes by one spouse screaming, "Rewards!" and the other screaming, "Risks!"

But who knows, you could become the next Bill Gates!

Author's Note

I e-mailed this chapter to some of my closest pals before the manuscript was finished. We do have a united campaign against our wives' party fever. Cracking the lid on this party circuit is a dangerous job, but hey, so is trying to make a living selling long distance. The author would like to thank Robert "Bob" Clippinger for his security-conscious contribution.

The e-mail reads—

Joey,

Got your chapter and was busy laughing until I got wind of the contract on your life by MOPS (Mothers of Preschoolers) International. If you publish this chapter in your book, I think you ought to use a pen name or else hire a bodyguard. You just broke the secret domain of female parties, and don't think for a moment that they will let you out alive. As a matter of fact, unless you stop publishing this radical material, I will no longer be able to associate with you . . . I have a family!!!!!

See you???

Bob

You Should Know How I Feel!

6

If you want your spouse to listen and pay strict attention to every word you say, talk in your sleep.

Let's face one important fact about men and women: It is impossible for women to know what men are thinking, and it is equally impossible for men to know what women are feeling. The chasm between understanding a man's world and a woman's world is so huge that universities are actually being formed to help married couples better understand one another.

In my research to better understand the psychosocialmentalchemicaltemperamental differences between men and women, I came across The Whatsamatta Online University at http://www.menarealwayswrong.com. Adhering to the rigorous academic standard of giving proper credit where credit is due, I found no source for the following information. Therefore, the author of this piece is recognized as anonymous. On second thought, he probably meant to do that. The university is offering the following courses for guys to better understand why the female mind gets so frustrated with men. Here are their top ten suggested classes:

1. The Remote Control—Overcoming Your Dependency

2. Romanticism—Other Ideas beyond Sex

3. How Not to Act Younger Than Your Children

4. You Cannot Always Wear Whatever You Please

5. We Do Not Want Sleazy Underwear for Christmas (Just Give Us Credit Cards)

6. The Weekend and Sports Are Not Synonymous

7. You, the Weaker Sex

8. Parenting Roles beyond Initial Conception

9. Get a Life—Learn to Cook

10. You Don't Look Like Mel Gibson, Especially When Naked

For women who wish to probe for signs of intelligent life in the minds of men, there was also another web site offered by The Whatsamatta Online University at *http://www.cantlivewithemcantlivewithoutem.com.* The University recommends the following ten courses for women:

1. Get a Life—Learn to Kill Spiders Yourself

2. You Can Change the Oil Too

3. Romanticism—The Whole Point of Caviar, Candles, and Conversation

4. Attainable Goal—Catching a Ball Before It Stops Moving

5. We Do Not Want Ties for Christmas (Just Wear the Sexy Lingerie I Gave You)

6. Payday and Shopping Are Not Synonymous

7. How to Do All Your Laundry in One Load and Have More Time to Watch Football

8. Why It Is Unacceptable to Talk about Feminine Hygiene in Mixed Company

9. It's Okay to Do It Outside of the Bedroom

10. How Not to Sob Like a Sponge When Your Husband Is Right

Attending universities to better understand what men are thinking and what women are feeling may offer some basic benefits in understanding the differences between the sexes, but in the following pages, I will offer you a simpler, less expensive, and authoritatively conclusive explanation for the true reasons why men and women are so different. There are no tests. No assignments. No fees. It's one of the many side benefits of buying my book.

After billions of dollars spent in scientific research, it has been concluded that it is impossible for men to understand what women are feeling. Despite what many women assume, men are not mind-readers. What many women do not know is that all guys have a hair-net-like web of nerves covering their entire brain called the "Intellectuous Maximus." The Intellectuous Maximus is not to be confused with intelligence. The Intellectuous Maximus does not determine a guy's level of intelligence, but simply shows *how he thinks and perceives events and interactions with people.* Including women.

According to Webster, the definition of *intellect* is "the

ability to reason or understand." Words associated with the Intellectuous Maximus that guys readily identify with are *logic, analysis, reasoning, critical, productive, assertive,* and *competitive.* Because of the Intellectuous Maximus covering their brain, guys think they know everything. And if a guy knows everything, how could he ever be wrong?

The origin of the Intellectuous Maximus goes back to cave person days when guys guarded and protected the camp. They spoke in monosyllabic grunts like they still do today. They hunted for saber-toothed tigers and fought off woolly mammoths who broke into car windows in search of Snickers candy bars. They scratched, picked, and played with their tools, crude implements of wood and stone made by the early founders of Black & Decker. It was basically hunt and grunt.

During one violent era, the entire human race was facing near-extinction due to daily airborne attacks from a particularly vicious group of pterodactyls. The peashooters that were an effective defense against the saber-toothed tigers and woolly mammoths were absolutely useless against the high-flying pterodactyls. Each day, men, women, and children were being whisked away in the jaws of the pterodactyls, who would take them to their caves for a light lunch. The series of cataclysmic events forced all the guys to put their brains together and come up with an emergency plan to save the camp.

It was the stress and urgency of this crisis that caused a physiological reaction in guys' brains and led to the subsequent development of the Intellectuous Maximus. The solution they arrived at was a sneak attack on the pterodactyl cave, whereby the few remaining cave guys jumped on the pterodactyls' backs, licked their index fingers, and proceeded to give the pterodactyls some serious wet willies. The pterodactyls were so grossed out that they forever lost their taste for humans.

At this same time, women were getting pretty frustrated with losing all their children to the vicious pterodactyls. After already having a few kids, the thought of being pregnant and overweight again spurred them to action. The Intuitive Minimus was developed out of frustration when cave women watched their husbands cuss and swear after banging their thumbs as they attempted to make new weapons that would never work against the vicious pterodactyls. Time and time again, the cave women tried to make helpful suggestions, but they were repeatedly stonewalled by their cave husbands who said, "No way—that'll never work. I know exactly what I'm doing."

The Intuitive Minimus is a purse-shaped chemical that travels freely about a woman's brain. To quote Webster again, the definition of *intuition* is "the immediate knowing of something without the conscious use of reasoning." Thus, since women already know what they need to know, they have no immediate need for logic or reasoning. The Intuitive Minimus prides itself on its cooperative, feeling, nurturing, receptive, flexible, and accepting characteristics. Unlike the rigid, fixed position of the Intellectuous Maximus, the Intuitive Minimus can easily travel to the heart and thus enable a woman to be in touch with her feelings. The Intuitive Minimus gives a woman exactly what she needs at the correct time and place to make the right decision. The Intellectuous Maximus needs a lot of concrete, logical information to make sure it's right, but the Intuitive Minimus needs very little information to produce that warm, gut-level feeling that confirms a woman's hunches. When a woman is right, *she's right,* and it is the Intuitive Minimus that confirms what she's feeling. Without having to be defensive, all a woman has to say to justify her position is, "I just know I'm right."

Faced with the terrifying thought of sleep deprivation and dealing with the terrible twos again, women gathered around the campfire and sketched out plans in the dirt for killing the vicious pterodactyls. They designed intricate pterodactyl radar warning systems, shoulder-launched Stinger missiles, anti-pterodactyl laser guns, and spring-loaded net catapults. By morning, they had the weapons built and ready to use against the vicious pterodactyls. Unfortunately, just then, the caveguys strolled into camp high-fiving one another and bragging about their wet willie sneak attack on the vicious pterodactyls. Not to be outdone, the cave women now had an easy target.

Common Ground

Have you ever thought of becoming a brain surgeon to better understand your spouse? Wouldn't it be a whole lot easier if your spouse thought and felt just like you? Wouldn't it be nice to avoid going to extremes simply by plugging your brain into your spouse's brain and downloading all the information you need to understand what they're thinking or feeling? If you're frustrated at your husband's lack of sensitivity for your feelings or if you're upset at your wife's attempt at brain surgery to figure out what you're thinking, remember that your spouse is not wired to think or feel like you.

Though men and women share similar qualities and characteristics, women do have a predisposition to be more intuitive and feeling-oriented than men. On the other lobe, men have the predisposition to be more reason- and logic-oriented than women. These predispositions, along with how men and women are socialized in our society, explain why men are the way they are and why women are the way they are. So, trying to *change* your husband or wife so they will better understand your wants and needs is next to impossible.

What you can do, though, is to first understand your spouse's wiring so you can better communicate what you want and need from them. Understanding and accepting the way your spouse is wired can help you avoid extremes. Here are some tools to get you onto the common ground of understanding how your spouse thinks and feels.

Study Your Spouse. I know it sounds kinda crazy, but if you want to better understand your spouse, you need to study how they think and feel. What types of words do they use in their vocabulary? How do they react to certain situations? How do they handle conflict? What are they responsive to? What makes them angry or defensive? When are they most happy or sad? What do they like to do? What do they hate to do? What motivates them? What do they find most frustrating?

By studying your spouse, you will build your knowledge base of understanding who they are as a person. Based on that knowledge, there will be certain things you will do and won't do to get along with them. Though no husband or wife will ever completely understand their mate, studying your spouse can help you grow to appreciate their unique qualities.

Look for Positive Qualities. There's a simple principle that affects how you interact with everyone you meet and know: If you look for the positive qualities in a person, you will find them. If you look for the negative qualities in a person, you will find negative qualities as well. Everybody has strengths and weaknesses, faults and assets. Don't allow your best energy to be drained by picking out your spouse's character flaws. Your marriage will land on common ground much sooner and will become much more enjoyable if you focus on your spouse's positive qualities.

Pay Attention to Feelings. Husbands and wives need to pay attention to each other's feelings because feelings are the spark plugs for igniting conflict. They're also the spark plugs for igniting compatibility, intimacy, and romance. Couples with growing, loving marriages are those that pay particular attention to each other's feelings.

Every day you experience all sorts of different feelings about your spouse. What you feel about how your spouse treats you affects how you treat them. Though you can't always make decisions based on your feelings, you can learn to better express your feelings to your spouse in an open, sensitive, and tactful way.

If your husband isn't open about his feelings, the last thing you want to do is push him to open up. If your wife is dying to know what's going on in your heart and mind, the quickest way to her heart may be opening up yours. If you can pay attention, and respect and appreciate your spouse's feelings, you will be building a bridge of intimacy. That's a whole lot better than trying to perform brain surgery on each other!

You're Driving Me Crazy

7

It seemed like only yesterday that I attended
bridal parties where we sat around on folding
chairs dressing clothespins in crepe paper and
hyperventilating when we won a spatula.
—Erma Bombeck

I don't get it—it takes weeks of practice, hundreds of dollars, hours of study, and a battery of written and practical tests to get a driver's license. To get a marriage license, all it takes is thirty-five bucks, a couple of signatures, and a squirt of blood. They say love is blind, but nobody even makes you take a vision test.

You pop the clutch during your driving test, you fail. You're a loser. That means you book yourself into DMV hell. You go to the end of a very long line of DMV sinners, and it'll be a very cold day before you ever get to the front of that big, long line. And no, none of your friends will be there with you.

You want to get married? You pop the question and people throw you parties. Engagement parties. Bridal showers. Bachelor parties. Friends and family get starry-eyed and fawn all over you like a newborn baby. People celebrate by taking you and your betrothed to dinner. The champagne bottle pops and you're the toast of the town. I don't know about you, but by the time I reached my wedding day, I was exhausted from all those parties.

Getting a driver's license is much harder than getting a marriage license. You slave away to earn the right to drive on America's greatest highways and what does the DMV do? Throw confetti? A party? Send you a Hallmark congratulations card in the mail? No way. They read you the riot act. Break the law and you're burnt toast. Exceed the speed limit and you go to DMV Purgatory, commonly known as traffic school. Traffic school is responsible for more deaths by boredom every year in the U.S. than all traffic fatalities worldwide. You also incur hefty fines and get points on your driving record, which the DMV loves because they secretly own all the auto insurance companies.

Drink and drive and you'll really be circling the drain. You get five thousand community service frequent-flier miles for free, a lifetime membership in AA (not to be confused with AAA), and a free map of the local bus routes in your town. And rightly so, the DMV has a reputation to protect.

I don't know about you, but the most dangerous days of my life were spent when I was packed into a tiny Ford Escort with two other nervous student drivers and our clipboard-toting driving instructor. After a dozen or so near-fatal misses and a sore neck from excessive student-driver brakeage, I came away with a sense of accomplishment and relief.

I survived.

I *earned* that driver's permit and that was only one step in a series of many state-mandated steps.

Getting a marriage license is easier than getting a driver's license. Way easier.

You and I live in a crazy world. Go figure. It's even easier to get a divorce than to get a point removed from your driving record.

Giving a sixteen-year-old a license to drive is practically giving them a license to kill, but getting a marriage license is like a deer applying for a hunting license. One makes you a killer on the road. The other makes you road kill.

Get engaged and all people talk about are dress sizes, wedding gowns, reception appetizers like salmon cheese loaf and duck pâté, friends and in-laws coming from out of town. But nobody mentions a word about cleaning up vomit at three A.M., or what the best strategies are for winning the silent game when you're in a fight, or how the things your fiancée loved to do with you before you got married—like watching ESPN, kissing a rugged unshaved face, or playing football with the guys—are now loathed.

And nobody ever tells you to kill your old life as you know it.

Yeah, guys will throw the old ball and chain around the ankle at the bachelor party, but what they really ought to give you is a straitjacket.

Marriage makes you crazy!

Ever since I got married, I have been a terminal idiot. Though some family members will argue that was my mental state before marriage, I do now have a keener understanding of the relationship between commitment and mental institutions. If you don't think marriage makes you crazy, look at what happens when husbands and wives tie the knot in each other's straitjacket.

I Need to Return a Few Things. Before women get married, they have nothing to return and no reason to return anything to any store in Anywhere, USA. The day a woman gets engaged, she begins accumulating. The day she gets back from her honeymoon, she begins liquidating. Three-quarters of the wedding gifts go back to the store. In fact, it takes a full two years before all your wedding gifts are exchanged for innocuous appliances that end up in the back of lower kitchen shelves you never see.

No, you don't need four rice makers, eight hibachi grills, or the dozens of other completely useless knickknacks that take on a life of their own in the garage sale circuit, but all of this taking-back stuff seems weird to a guy. Most guys don't understand how this behavior early in the marriage leads to further shopping extremes down the road.

Take, for example, what happens when you have kids.

The day after your first baby shower, your wife became an official "returnaholic." Through each developmental stage of your children's growth (it's not over, I warn you), your wife will buy . . . return, buy . . . return, buy . . . return like a crazy woman. That is, unless your wife is one of those women who are mortified at the thought of returning anything. In cases like this, a woman *feels* bad about how her third-cousin-once-removed would *feel* if she ever found out that her thoroughly useless child-safe Chia Pet was returned. Second, your wife would feel additional guilt and angst over how the saleslady might *feel* because your wife inconvenienced her by returning the perfectly child-safe Chia Pet. Last, your wife would *feel* even more terrible about hogging a whole parking spot at the mall. Every woman knows how hard it is to find a parking spot, and your wife is not going to take one without a very good reason.

Once your wife starts returning things, she then will have every reason to return anything at any moment anywhere in the USA. She will spend at least half of your married life returning things. Receipts are her sacred scrip. She will put more mileage on your car by driving ten miles to the mall and back than circumnavigating the globe. Knowing what you know now, my sage advice for all husbands is to buy stock in oil companies.

Believe me, when a woman has to return something to a store, there is always a strong reason. Not a clear, logical, or sound reason, perhaps. Just a strong reason.

It doesn't feel right.

It doesn't match.

There's a new sale. I can get my money back and buy more.

It makes me look like a bloated whale.

I don't like it.

This circular shopping behavior is extreme and it drives me crazy. I'm willing to endow a fellowship for anyone crazy enough to study it.

Hey, You're Not Throwing That Out—I Like That! If women have a bent for returning anything with a price tag on it, men are equally wired to hang on to any item that serves no useful purpose in married life. After the honeymoon, not only do women liquidate the wedding gifts they don't like, they also liquidate all of the post-bachelor items their husbands are trying to hang on to. These items are anything—*I repeat*—anything relating to his possessions or decorating skills as a bachelor. Down to his very toothbrush. If he is adamant about wanting to keep the Incredible Hulk toothbrush he's had since he was eight years old, his new bride will break into tears and throw the gift-wrapped his and hers toothbrush set at him that she was dying to surprise him with.

Men drive their wives crazy when they try to keep old Naugahyde couches, eviscerated recliner chairs, Ferrari posters with contorted women lying on the hood, foreign beer collections, assorted silverware from three different thrift stores, any comfortable sweats or T-shirts left over from college, and Cup O' Noodles.

The moment a guy and his new bride pull away for the honeymoon, the Salvation Army truck pulls into the driveway. It is sweet salvation for the new bride and a bitter departure of all things a guy holds dear. Beg and plead as he may, bachelor junk drives married women crazy, so it's not hard to see why so many men have an ethical dilemma when their wives say, "Either that ugly couch goes or I go."

I still can't figure out what my wife saw wrong with my set of high-quality, brown ceramic plates and matching coffee mugs I got at a garage sale in college. They worked great. Hey, they were kiln fired!

Common Ground

Because marriage is such an extreme state, of course it leads you and your beloved to all sorts of extremes. When you bellow at your spouse, "You're driving me crazy," you both are well on the road to marital insanity. Since it is so easy to acquire a marriage license, to ensure harmony in the home, tighter marriage guidelines must be established to prevent each person from going wacko. Couples who follow these guidelines during marriage will no doubt experience some degree of sanity and sense of personal dignity.

Guideline #1: Nobody Held a Gun to Your Head. Except for some parts of the Ozarks, shotgun weddings are passé in America today. It's amazing how, in a relatively short time, a person can claim that the man or woman they were crazy about before they got married is now the same person who is driving them crazy. We live with our choices even if our choices have halitosis and foot odor strong enough to start a stampede. But what about the people who say they no longer love their spouses and claim, "I was a fool and in love"? Let's look at it this way: if the person who uses this line is no longer in love, where does that leave them?

We'd better not go there.

You are a different person today from the day you chose to marry your spouse just as your spouse is a different person today from the day he or she chose to marry you. The trick to a good marriage is to keep choosing to love your mate each day you're married. You can adjust to the changes of life and the changes in your marriage by choosing to continue loving your spouse even when they do drive you crazy. Choosing to love is one choice you'll never regret.

Guideline #2: Get a Sense of Humor. Before your spouse sends you to the nut house, why not look at his or her foibles, idiosyncrasies, eccentricities, and obsessions with a sense of humor? Couples who keep a sense of humor in marriage stay on the common ground of laughter and joy. Laughter is about the only extreme people don't get sick of, and it is a crucial ingredient in a happy marriage.

Taking yourself or your spouse too seriously is a dead-end road. Far too many couples get lost in their marriage because they lose their sense of humor. They allow their sense of spontaneity and playfulness to slip. When you can't laugh at yourself or laugh with your spouse about the crazy things you both do, that's when real dementia sets in. If you're serious as a heart attack, you just may have one. You can put the sanity back in your marriage by getting a sense of humor and giving your spouse the delirious gift of laughter.

Guideline #3: Keep Moving Forward. One of the best ways to keep a marriage moving forward is by having faith in

God and faith in your spouse. That's risky business, but it'll definitely keep your marriage alive and growing. A lot of marriages get off common ground because the common ground the marriage is built on becomes boring and predictable. Instead of moving forward to new adventures like pioneers in a covered wagon, the homestead becomes like a decaying swamp.

If you encourage your husband or wife to try and do new things, you will be stimulating personal growth that will pay dividends in your marriage. Start a new hobby. Take ballroom dancing together. Go to a cooking or photography class. Try a new sport. Send her on a trip alone with girlfriends. Read in a new genre or write a song.

If you also encourage your spouse to have faith in God and participate together in faith-building activities like attending church, reading Scripture, praying together, and serving others less fortunate than yourself, you both will always have something to talk about. Love, laughter, and faith—what a great way to drive each other crazy.

I Can't Believe You Just Did That!

8

In America, marriage is the only legal method of suppressing freedom of speech.

I'm sorry, sir, the car's been sold. Your wife just signed the pink slip and it's a done deal."

"Whoa! Whoa! Whoa! Whoa!" I stammered as a small, skinny guy dressed in Levi's and a flannel shirt walked toward *my car* holding *my car keys* and the pink slip to *my car* in his hand.

I had just pulled into our driveway and gotten out of Krista's car to witness what had to be an illegal transaction. No, my wife wasn't selling drugs—she was selling my car. Something was definitely wrong with this picture.

I almost bellowed a Fred Flintstone–Wilma cry, "KRIS-TA!" to demand clarification about the exchange that had just taken place. My gut felt that hollow, achy, sinking, quicksand feeling, which is nature's signal in crisis situations confirming what we already know to be true. My head also realized what had just happened, but like the cerebral cortex in many male brains, it was just playing stupid until all the facts were in.

Dazed, I asked Krista, "What's going on here?" A safe, information-gathering question.

"You didn't sell my car did you?" An obviously dumb question to which I did not want a response, at least in the affirmative.

"Look, he paid us in cash," Krista responded with a hint of "uh-oh" in her voice.

I had a pained, confused look on my face. The furrows on my forehead were deeper than the Grand Canyon and my contorted body language looked like I'd suffered dearly in a Twister competition. (Twister by Hasbro, that is.)

My gut taunted my head, "Told you so! Told you so!"

"Now, wait a minute," I barked at the guy with my keys. (I now know why "Cash for Autos" salesmen, repo guys, and people who serve lawsuits have very dangerous jobs; we were definitely not on the same team.) *This car is not sold. I didn't sign anything—you can't just take my car like that.*"

"Oh yes, I can, sir. Your wife signed the pink slip and the sale papers. I just paid her cash and the car is sold. It happens like this all the time. Now, sir, can I get you to remove your things from the car?"

Visualize rage. Again.

Wives, does your husband ever get so irate that all his words seem to blend into one long, unintelligible sentence like "I-can't-believe-pst-ftd-this-is-actually-happening-pst-fdah-ugh!"

Men, if your wife ever wants to swap cars with you for the day, make sure you've got the pink slip in your pocket. That tip alone is worth the price of this book. I just saved you five hundred bucks.

When Krista sold my car, my response was like a combined epileptic seizure, heart attack, elephantiasis, demon possession, and a case of salmonella poisoning. To put it mildly.

Okay, I admit, it was only a two-door Toyota Corolla.

My first and only Toyota Corolla. Ever.

Yes, Krista and I had talked about selling it the week earlier, but did that give her the green light to go ahead and sell it? If you're a woman reading this, don't you dare nod your head and say, "Yes."

Guys, I had to sign a major public disclosure spousal security clearance to write this chapter. I promised to authentically represent all aspects of the situation from each vantage point. From Krista's perspective, she thought that since we had both agreed to sell the car, she could then go ahead and sell it. In fairness, the day she sold my car to that parasitical leech, she did try to call me first, but was unable to reach me.

There.

I had no idea she had active plans to sell the car. If there's one thing guys hate, it's being kept out of the loop in major financial decisions like selling cars, houses, and premarital bachelor heirlooms like old sofas and the complete 7-Eleven NFL Slurpee Cup Collector's set. I can even make a case for the family financial ramifications of selling lemon bars at a PTA fund-raiser.

So when Krista sold my used Corolla that had a mismatched paint job and peeling window tint, as you can imagine, I went ballistic. I was so livid-incensed-chapped-raw-furious-piqued-inflamed-enraged-toddlerish-provoked-and-annoyed, I coulda spit nails.

Yes, I was the founder of MADD, Men Against Disturbing Decisions.

By nature, men are pretty reserved with their emotions. It goes back to the guarding-the-camp thing. Men are cautious. Suspicious. Wary. Especially among car thieves, um, I mean, honest and ethical used-car dealers who come to homes and prey on women with pink slips and their husbands' Toyota Corollas.

I'm not bitter.

Really.

Except for passionate surges in Italian, Latin, or Irish blood, most Caucasian men in America have a cooler, let's-not-get-too-excited-and-have-a-heart-attack-over-nothing, WASPy emotional orientation.

Not me. I'm a Mick. I go a hundred percent both sides back to dee windswept pastures of me Irish Faderland. I don't get mad often, but when I get mad, I wear my angry body language like a GI Joe uniform.

Anger isn't gender-specific. Women have as much a proclivity for anger as men do. Especially when their husbands are late coming home from work. Late in calling when they said they would call. Late in arriving at children's school events. Late in reading obvious mating signals when she is ovulating.

A wife can also get ticked off when a guy's idea of romance on Valentine's Day is sharing a box of greasy, lukewarm chicken at the Monster Truck Rally. Or when he is sacrificially thinking of her before himself by buying her season tickets to the Chicago Bulls. Or when he comes home from work, the family dog gets more hugs-n-kisses-n-squeezes-n-pats-on-the-behind than she does. Or when she's forced to stare into a crystal ball in order to read what's going on in his mind.

When you are flaming mad at your spouse, anger is one of those rare emotions that acutely reminds you that you are indeed married.

Common Ground

This is a book about extremes. Anger is one of those extremes on the emotional scale of life that most men and women don't handle very well. Any couple that is reasonably honest with one another knows how easy it is to go from warm "mad about you" feelings of love and affection to those ferocious "I'm mad at you—don't you dare get near me" savage-like feelings of disdain, distance, and disgust.

Webster gives a great definition for *anger*. He probably defined the word in the midst of a fight with his wife. He says anger is "hostile feelings because of opposition." He's darn right! Exactly my point. You get angry at your spouse when he or she *opposes* your thoughts, feelings, needs, desires, wants, and ideas. The opposition of your spouse frustrates your plans, blocks your wishes, and dashes your expectations. That opposition is what causes you and your spouse to go to extremes.

Women are always right and men are never wrong when they oppose one another like the main event on a hot Spanish afternoon. Your husband may be a raging bull with size, strength, and sharp horns for protection, but what *matadora* would walk into a ring without a cape, spear, and sword? Every couple knows how to hurt one another by attacking the other person's vulnerabilities, weaknesses, character flaws, and bad habits.

And anger in the heart, this volatile emotion that is a very real part of our emotional makeup, is what precedes the damaging words and actions we use to hurt our spouse.

Some people believe that anger is a sin and that it's wrong to be angry over anything. Well, if that's true, then God must be a sinner because over and over in the Bible, God gets angry over all sorts of things. The right things. Other people think, *Well, if I really loved my spouse, I would never be angry at him or her.* Wrong again. Look in any phone book and you'll discover that marriage counselors are listed right next to martial arts studios. Coincidence? I don't think so.

Anger is a God-given emotion that serves as a red flag that something is obviously wrong and needs to be dealt with. The appropriate use of anger in a marriage can be great evidence of gut-level honesty and vulnerability that says, "Why are you opposing me? I want to be one with you, but we can't until this issue gets dealt with!" Anger can be a great motivator to resolve issues by creating defining moments of truth-telling in the marriage relationship. If both parties are willing to deal with the problem, that is.

Sounds clean and antiseptic, I know. Unfortunately, anger is a messy emotion. By its very nature, it usually creates more trouble and trauma than healing and wholeness. The tornado always comes before the truce.

If you're angry at your spouse, especially because he or she won't read this book with you, admit it. There's nothing to be gained by denying your anger and later spending thousands of dollars in therapy trying to remember what you were angry about. Admitting your anger over whatever issue you're dealing with is one of the first steps to resolving it. And even if the issue can't be resolved immediately or it's one you and your spouse have been wrestling over for some time, admitting your anger will at least emotionally orient you to where your feelings truly are.

Think about how you handle your anger. Do you go to extremes and come out swinging like a boxer instead of thinking through the consequences of your words and actions? Do you stuff your anger and play the Silent Game by expecting your spouse to know what's wrong? Do you yell and scream? Do you fight fair and stick to the issue at hand, or do you bring up past offenses and grievances as ammo for your verbal machine gun? Do you pout, whine, complain, or manipulate instead of telling the truth about how you're really feeling? Do you rally the troops of your kids, friends, or family members to build consensus against your opponent—er—spouse?

Every person has a different way of handling anger. Perhaps it might be useful for you and your spouse to establish some common ground by talking about how you both would like to see anger handled in an appropriate way in your relationship. What words and actions hurt your spouse when you're angry? What are some simple ways to deal with a problem before it escalates into a Mount St. Helens eruption? Think and talk about the stuff that makes you angry—when you're not angry of course.

And please exercise some self-control on my behalf—don't blame me if this conversation about anger starts a fight between the two of you. I know this is a dangerous chapter. I already feel like an oxymoron just using anger and self-control in the same sentence.

You should've seen me when Krista sold my car.

You Never Put the Toilet Seat Down

9

How many men does it take to change a roll of toilet paper?
We don't know—it's never happened.

If sex begins in the kitchen, then marriage battles begin in the bathroom. True, most couples prefer making love to making war, but the bathroom of almost every American couple is flush with vivid examples of the extremes men and women go to over the silliest of arguments.

Most marital disagreements—er, *discussions*—begin with ridiculous spats over one forgetful spouse neglecting to return the toothpaste cap to its original airtight position on the tube where it belongs. Feeling unjustly attacked for wasting a dried-out sliver of dentist-preferred Crest, the accused spouse counters with a snide or sarcastic remark about a specific forgetful habit or misdeed of said accuser. Soon, a fierce war of words, flying gobs of toothpaste, dental floss nooses, and caustic threats of *"Back! I have a Water Pik and I know how to use it,"* send the warring couple into separate sleeping quarters.

All over a stupid toothpaste cap.

Another silly fight that begins in the bathroom deals with hair. Razor stubble left like foamy dirt in the sink. Clumps of body hair amassed in bas-relief in the bathtub. Tangles of long, sodden hair clogging the shower drain. Let's face a simple fact: Men and women are hairy, but it's tough to say who is the most follicle-impaired. If you're bald and reading this paragraph, you'll be glad to know I won't be making any bald jokes. I've seen all the hair commercials and Plug-a-Rug ads that say, "Hair loss is not a laughing matter." I take those very seriously.

Ever since childhood, modern man has learned from shaving commercials that true manhood is derived from a clean shave. Shaving is one of the few rites of passage left to men in an increasingly complex and technological world. It is a rare link between a man's childhood and the childish behavior he is capable of displaying even as an adult. A guy, who can also be referred to as the man-child, is reminded of this important rite of passage almost every day he shaves.

Nobody said anything about cleaning the sink!

What sailor ever did *that* on the Old Spice aftershave commercials?

When failing to clean the ant farm of whiskers left in the foam-laced sink, the man-child enters a new marital rite of passage by hearing touching terms of endearment like "Slob," "Shower Scum," "Pig," and "Vermin." This language confuses the man-child, who also has more chest, back, and overall body hair than the average women. Shaving, not cleaning the sink, is what is tied to his innermost psyche. Any comment, whether well-intentioned or well-aimed by the man-child's mate, is perceived as an attack not on his whiskers, but on his very manhood. Can he help it, he also reasons, that when he dries himself in the shower, he sheds like a spitting Peruvian alpaca?

With a little coaching and prodding and a complete body shave after being drugged, the man-child can learn how to clean the shower and sink. But many wives will find this to be a frustrating experience. Like alpacas, the man-child is one of the worst animals to train.

Male and female plumbers alike will confirm that women with long hair can clog shower and bathtub drains, thus necessitating the need for the Roto-Rooter man or a gallon of Liquid-Plumr. Women also shave their legs and under their arms (in America), but usually in the bath or shower. Everybody knows that bath and shower water volume is greater than the volume of sink water. For women, this accounts for a smooth stubble flow down the drain. This is where men are at a disadvantage. They must strategically plan to dispose of their hair waste accordingly or rid themselves of their Old Spice understanding of how the world really works.

I don't want to split hairs over this next bathroom battle husbands and wives get into, but my personal favorite is the toilet seat argument. The bottom line is this—

Women are always saying, "You never put the toilet seat back down."

Au contraire . . . women never put the seat back up.

When a man and woman get married, the first fight occurs sometime during the honeymoon when the unsuspecting bride gets a gravity flush by falling backward into the toilet bowl. She is now hurt, embarrassed, and really ticked off at her moron goon—er, *groom*—who forgot to put the toilet seat back down. Though seriously concerned about his new bride's backside injuries, the guy might as well forget about sex for the next week. Or at least until he gets toilet trained.

The thing that drives us guys crazy about the whole toilet seat deal is this: If guys must put the toilet seat back down, how come women never have to raise it back up? Women, who are always right, argue that a toilet seat always belongs in the down position. Who says? The hinge works both ways. Whether you are standing or sitting, it's all a matter of perspective.

By raising the toilet seat, women do have the forces of gravity working against them. A lot of energy is expended raising that two-ton toilet seat back into the upright position. It belongs down, they reason, so why bother?

On the other hand, men do have gravity working on their side, so they really don't have a good excuse for not lowering the lid. But guys are faced with a complete double standard here (not to be confused with American Standard or Swisher: A Publicly Traded Company): Guys are required to do double duty by first raising the seat and, once they are finished doing their duty, again lowering the seat so their unsuspecting wife, daughter, or houseguest doesn't do a backflip into the bowl. It's not a widely reported fact, but did you know that last year over four hundred thousand men in the United States, while attempting to be polite and considerate, were injured due to toilet seats smacking their kneecaps on the way down?

This brings me to an ancillary story. Ellie, our three-year-old daughter, is a TP protégée. The other day she screams from the potty, "Daaaddddeee! I neeeed toyyylet paper!"

So I go into the bathroom and Ellie's sitting there, legs dangling back and forth, doing her toddler toilet thing. I put the paper on the roller. She carefully examines my technique. When I'm finished, she critiques my changing of the roll duties and proclaims in her most authoritative sanitation engineer voice, "Daddy, you put the roll on backward."

Ugh!

I immediately walked over to Krista in the kitchen and demanded, "What are you teaching this child? How does a three-year-old know how the toilet paper is supposed to go on the roll?"

Krista professed innocence, stating she's taught Ellie absolutely nothing about the correct way to put on toilet paper, though she did agree that Ellie was right about the TP placement and I was wrong. Again. Future research will deem that it is an inherent female trait to place toilet paper so that it hangs down in front, thus ensuring an adequate forward grasp with a simple turn of the roll. I already know what Martha Stewart would say.

Men, we know, put paper on so that it rolls from the back. Rolling from the back ensures a better roll in terms of speed and quantity. Yes, it's harder to grab, it sometimes gets stuck in the back, but hey, we like a challenge. Even when we are reprimanded by three-year-olds.

Common Ground

If you think arguing over toothpaste caps, toilet seats, or toilet paper placement is extreme, what about all the other silly arguments we get into with our spouses?

Marriage is like a prize fight without the money. If you and your spouse learn how to successfully work through and resolve conflict, the prize you've both earned will be a satisfying and rewarding marriage. Couples who don't take the time to understand and appreciate each other's differences and work through their problems only do damage to each other, their marriage, and their family.

I'm convinced that couples need to be able to laugh with one another over all the wild extremes and conflicts they go through over the course of their married lives. That includes laughing about the things we fight about. When in the heat of battle, we all know fights in marriage aren't a laughing matter. But when things settle down, humor helps to expose our humanness as we work through the conflicts that are a part of every marriage.

Fighting is one of those extremes in marriage no couple can get away from. Every couple fights and those who say they don't are delusional individuals who probably work as cash-for-auto salesmen. I read one quote from a lady in severe denial who said, "We don't fight; we negotiate." I don't want to bicker and dicker over semantics, but we know that lawyers also don't fight: They negotiate. No matter what spin you put on it, fighting is fighting.

Hopefully, fighting isn't a huge part of your marriage, but fighting is as real an issue in marriage as any other issue. How you and your spouse handle your conflicts and disagreements says a lot about you as an individual and as a couple. Couples who accept each other's differences, establish common ground rules for fighting, and learn to work through conflict will develop stronger, more fulfilling marriages.

You entered your marriage with your own unique personality, temperament, thoughts, feelings, opinions, family history, dreams, goals, likes and dislikes, hurts and struggles, talents and abilities, and way of thinking. So did your spouse. Many of the unique characteristics and differences you both found attractive in one another are the common ground on which you built your marriage. Those unique characteristics and differences are also the common ground you go to war on.

Fighting is often a sign of a healthy marriage. Fighting says that there are two people in this marriage and not one. Since marriage is an extremely long commitment, fighting is one of those necessary vital signs that can indicate life and growth if conflicts are resolved in a healthy way. When differences aren't resolved, fighting can also signal the ebbing pulse of the marriage and its eventual decay.

So what are helpful common ground rules for forging through fights? Growing up in the home of a funeral director, I learned a thing or two about burying people. Marriage is the last place you want to bury your conflicts while they're still kicking. Burying conflict only breeds hidden anger, resentment, and animosity. *Don't bury unresolved conflict.*

Next, once the deceased conflict is buried, don't resurrect it as ammo for future fights. It's difficult for a spouse to change for the better if the other spouse is always dredging up past behavior. Stick to the current issue and not remotely related ones.

As much as I hate to say it, avoid the words "You always—" and "You never—." Those words are extremes. Rarely are they based in reality. They'll put your spouse on the defensive and cause 'em to dig in more. Instead, use middle-of-the-road language by speaking for yourself. For example, "I feel hurt when such and such happens—." Speak for yourself and how you feel, not for your spouse and what he or she did.

Last, when there is no conflict, sit down and develop your own common ground rules for dealing with and resolving conflict in your marriage. For the sake of each other and your marriage, make it your mutual goal to resolve every conflict. When you both get on common ground for resolving the inevitable fights that are necessary for the growth and health of your marriage, you both win.

There is one battle, however, I know I can't win. I don't dare venture into the "folding" or "scrunching" toilet paper debate.

I choose my battles very carefully.

What I Hear You Saying Is—

10

The Japanese sport of judo is the art of conquering by yielding. The Western equivalent is saying, "Yes, dear."

did you hear about the recent study that reveals how to have a happy marriage? Wives, you're *really* going to like the results of this study. Guys, it should be nothing new to you, but please activate your ears to hear what I'm saying—

Conducted by University of Washington Professor Dr. John Gottman, the study found that the traditional pop counseling technique of "active listening" was used very infrequently by couples to resolve conflicts. The study also found that using active listening was no predictor of marital success.

I couldn't agree more. Have you ever tried active listening?

Say you and your wife are in the midst of an argument while driving downtown for a quiet dinner together. Your argument goes something like this—

HUSBAND: I said I didn't care what we had for dinner tonight. I'm so hungry I'll eat anything.

WIFE: That's the problem—you don't care! How often do we get a night out alone without the kids? This is supposed to be a date! You're supposed to take a little more initiative and find a restaurant we both like.

HUSBAND: *Watch out, honey! You're drifting into the oncoming lane!*

WIFE: You're right; I should watch my words and not drift off into other issues. I'll start over—*what I hear you saying* is that you don't care about the quality of food we eat—whether it's Alpo, Gravy Train, or Purina Puppy Chow. If I hear you correctly, you don't care if both of us get the *E. coli* bacteria, right, dear? Tell me if what I repeated is what I think you said that I heard you say which I then repeated back to you—

HUSBAND: *Pull back into the right lane—there's a semi headed right for us!*

WIFE: Okay, let me repeat what I just heard you say— you're implying that you're semi-concerned about the type of food I put into my body. You know I have a proclivity for Hostess Twinkies, but—

HUSBAND: *That semi's lookin' bigger every second—do something!*

WIFE: What I heard you say is that I should do something about my figure and I agree with you. I've tried Jenny Craig food, but I can't stand how it tastes like sump tank seepage. I recently did cut back to skim chocolate milk and low-fat Oreos, but—

HUSBAND: *TURN THE WHEEL NOW OR WE'RE BOTH GONNA DIE!*

I'm glad someone finally debunked the active listening technique. It's awkward and unnatural, and when used with the proper German accent, it makes couples sound like amateur Freudian shrinks. Active listening does not lead to conflict resolution any more than defensive driving leads to semi truckers yielding the right of way.

In our house, what works much better is *reactive listening*.

My wife gets home from shopping and our conversation goes something like this—

WIFE: You wouldn't believe the sale they had at the craft store.

HUSBAND: Which means you bought twice as much?

WIFE: Exactly! Look at all this stuff I can make gifts out of—it was seventy-five percent off.

HUSBAND: How much?

WIFE: And look at these decorative potted plants I also got—they were so cheap!

HUSBAND: How much?

WIFE: Well, they weren't that much, but I haven't factored in the rental space we're going to need to store it all. Or maybe you could just build us a shed?

HUSBAND: How much?

WIFE: Well, I was thinking that since I got all of this for seventy-five percent off, I could give some away as gifts and then sell the rest at the Christmas boutique next November. Then, the profit I make from the boutique will pay off the cost of the shed.

HUSBAND: *Cuánto cuesta?*

Reactive listening keeps a good conflict right on course. All it needs is one spouse who isn't listening and the other spouse who's just reacting. Of course, if you do want to resolve conflict in your marriage, the aforementioned study revealed what guys have known since Adam gave in to Eve and ate the apple.

Dr. Gottman's conflict resolution technique, which is a predictor for a long and happy marriage, is known as "caving." Not to be confused with spelunking, caving is the process by which a man "caves in" to his wife during an argument and thus, by caving, allows her to win.

Guys, if you want a happy marriage according to Dr. Give-In, you gotta cave.

Now, when I first read this study, I had a lot of problems with its findings. It gave me pause to consider if I should do what my wife said and change the title of this book to *Women Are Always Right and Men Are Always Wrong,* but then I thought, *No way! We've had no argument about the title so the title stays!*

I didn't cave and I still have a happy marriage. So there!

Dr. Gonna-Get-a-Lotta-Hate-Mail-from-Noncompliant-Husbands says that a compliant husband, i.e., the caver, is the one who will have a happy marriage amid the wreckage of those couples who've tried to resolve conflict through active listening. Now you know the real origins of the words *cave man.*

Let the woman always be right? A happy marriage is a caving marriage? Conflict resolution means the collapse of the male ego? That's a bit radical. A lot of guys out there would choose running with the bulls over caving to their wives. This strikes at the core of a man's need for control, power, dominion, strength, and desire never to be wrong. The ramifications are frightening—

Does caving mean giving up the remote?

YEEESSS!!! cries Dr. Spineless-Jellyfish's all-female radio listening audience.

Does caving mean my wife is always right and I'm always wrong?

YES AGAIN! YES AGAIN! screams Dr. Gotta-Lotta-Nerve's nationwide following of Freed Females for Dr. Death-of-Everything-a-Man-Knows. The Freed Females begin to mock their husbands by chanting, "CAVE MAN! CAVE MAN! CAVE MAN!"

Once and for all, women are always right and world peace is achieved.

The battle of the sexes is officially over.

Couples never fight again. For this, Dr. Gottman is awarded the Nobel Peace Prize, hits the tabloid talk show circuit, and appears on the cover of *People* magazine with gorgeous supermodels and their mute cave-man husbands.

Common Ground

Maybe Dr. Gottman didn't use the *cave* word to describe what men must do to have a happy marriage, but he did use the word *influence,* and here, I think Dr. G. is onto something. He said that husbands who were willing to accept influence from their wives in dealing with marriage issues and conflicts were those that had the happiest marriages.

As I interviewed different couples for this book, a number of men (who will remain anonymous to protect the not-so-innocent) agreed that their wives were right more often than they were willing to admit. Hear me loud and clear: It doesn't mean their wives were right about everything. However, I've observed that guys who aren't worried about losing their manhood by letting their wives be right find themselves in bed with their wife where they belong rather than sleeping on the couch. It's a simple principle: Husbands and wives who are willing to accept each other's influence will be able to cut their losses a whole lot quicker than couples who are stuck in the defenses of their opinions and the pride of their positions.

This is a tough principle for a lot of guys to accept. Guys hate to cave. By nature, guys are competitive and they don't like to lose or lose control. They like to be strong, directive, and powerful. Losing an argument is ego-deflating and like a kidney punch to their pride. Our society has taught guys to take control, keep control, and never give up control. Some guys fear that if they cave in one area of control to their wives, then they'll have to cave in other areas as well. This unhealthy need for control is what keeps many guys from experiencing greater happiness in their marriage.

Women, on the other hand, are much more relational, cooperative, and wholistic. Although there are women who can be just as controlling as men, many women simply prefer to be *included* in decisions that affect them and the rest of the family. If a guy can allow himself not to be threatened by his wife's opinions, ideas, influence, and perspective, his cooperation will make him a more attractive husband.

If you're a guy reading this and you're having trouble accepting your wife's ideas and influence in your life, you can take a whole lot of pressure off yourself by allowing yourself to cooperate with your wife. Lighten up on yourself, will ya? If you're trying to keep your world together by constantly controlling it, you're only making life more difficult on yourself and your marriage. Your wife isn't impressed by your ability to keep it all together if it means she's excluded from having a significant say in what matters to her and her marriage.

Women want to be included. Learn this and you'll have a happier marriage.

But caving, or should I say "accepting influence" or "yielding," goes both ways. Too many couples experience unnecessary headaches and heartaches in their marriages because they are unwilling to accept each other's influence. Like two converging drivers who refuse to yield the right of way, each person is injured by the ensuing crash. Being unwilling to accept your spouse's ideas and influence in resolving the conflicts in your marriage keeps you both off common ground. Is that what's best for you? Your spouse? Your marriage?

Common ground is even ground. The goal in marriage is not to forcefully exert your influence on your spouse, but to gently accept his or her influence in your life. That means heeding, valuing, and accepting his or her thoughts, ideas, and opinions. Do you want to be on common ground, or do you want to spend your life in your own little control tower? Instead of creating chaos, isn't it easier to say to your spouse, "You know—you're right. I don't have to go to the mat on this one. You decide what's best and I'll support whatever you decide."

Giving up control may require a shift in the balance of power in your relationship, but you'll develop a more powerful and satisfying marriage as a direct result. By sharing power, both you and your spouse will become people of influence. Your mutual influence will strengthen each other and your marriage.

Ask yourself, "Am I open to my spouse's influence? Am I in my own control tower or do I cooperate with my spouse? Am I a controlling husband? Am I an unyielding wife? Do I seek my spouse's input? Do our fights go on and on because I refuse to yield? What are the issues in my marriage where I dig in and won't budge? What would this marriage be like if we both accepted each other's influence more often? What is the relationship between yielding to God and yielding to my spouse?"

These are tough questions, I know. Marriage is the mirror in which we see the best of ourselves and the worst of ourselves. The good news is that we have a God who is patient and compassionate and kind. He's also a God who's in control and likes to keep it that way. Accept His influence in your life. Yield to his Holy Spirit in your marriage. Follow His Son's example of giving up control.

Do these things and you'll become a very influential person.

Why Can't You Be Like Me?

11

Why can't a woman be more like a man?
—Henry Higgins, Pygmalion

A lot of intensive research went into this book. I interviewed brave couples willing to offer their marriages as fodder for my warped sense of humor. I surfed the Internet only to discover that the marriage of computers and telephone lines can be a tremendous waste of time, except for getting the daily surf report. Most important, I visited the vast halls of knowledge in the inner sanctums of used book stores. Here I found a long-lost treasury of previously unrecognized works on marriage. How these books never made the *New York Times* bestseller list astounds me!

On these dusty bookshelves, I discovered a clever little book entitled *You Too Can Have a Happy Husband,* which we all know should have had the subtitle *And You Too Can Keep Dreaming!*

Next, I wanted to frame this title: *Life with Women and How to Survive It.*

Another one I pulled off the shelf needs no explanation: *Please Read This for Me.*

If the coauthors were really honest, they would have titled the book *Please Read This for Me or Else!*

I did find a rare second edition, 1950s era masterpiece called *Personal Adjustment, Marriage, and Family Living.* If you're married with children, you don't need a chiropractor to figure that one out. This Ward Cleaver tome was filled with Ozzie & Harriet photos of guys in butch haircuts and women looking like Richie Cunningham's mom.

Hey, I learned a lot from that book.

There is a chapter about quarreling that you should read once you're finished with this book. Listen to this gem— "Many couples who have been married long enough to have celebrated a few anniversaries *seldom or never quarrel.* Their quarrels are in the past."

Wa-wa-wa-what?

The author was obviously single.

My personal favorite, though, was a landmark book that will help women understand once and for all why men act the way they do: *Apes & Husbands: From the Treetops to Today.*

Dismayed at what was happening to marriages all around him, author Frank Klock was determined to get to the fundamentals of the male/female relationship, so he started to study the higher apes—gorillas—just in case we may be related to them. No joke, good ol' Frank designed and built his own pocket, no-light microfilming camera and wound up with eight thousand shots of gorillas, which he analyzed and studied as the basis of his findings.

Poor Frank. He could have gone to an Angels game and taken one picture of forty thousand gorillas in a single shot.

Would've saved himself a ton of film and a few trips to Africa. Mr. Klock was obviously deprived as a child and never saw *Planet of the Apes.*

What I found most interesting was Mr. Klock's autobiographical information. Evidently, he married an Argentine lady (get this) of Basque-Inca descent, who was also a remote descendant of Atahualpa, last of the Inca emperors. So why is Frank picking on men? Why didn't he study his wife's Incan ancestors and call his book, *Apes & Atahualpa*? But noooo, he's gotta pick on men.

Mr. Klock did make one helpful observation. He documented that the gibbon is the most monogamous of all apes. This information is useful for single women who want to avoid marrying a philandering gorilla. Your gibbon will be hairy and not very human, but by gosh, he'll be faithful.

The one thing all these books shared in common was the profound insight that men and women are different. Unique. They think, perceive, act, talk, and respond to situations in different ways. This was a major revelation to me. A startling breakthrough. I'm sure it is to you as well.

Ever since puberty, I've always wondered why girls never grew facial hair. On my first day of school during my sophomore year of high school, I felt much better when I discovered my English teacher, Mrs. Buonaguidi, had a beard and mustache that put Grizzly Adams to shame. I'm sure she's now making beaucoup bucks selling her five o'clock shadow to the Men's Hair Club.

In my research, I also learned that men and women are different in every cell of their bodies. Evidently, some chromosomes began dating in order to find suitable mates. The guy chromosome always said he'd call, but never did. One particular female chromosome decided men are jerks and that she'd had enough. She put her foot down (X), and men have never had another leg to stand on since (Y).

It's a good thing that the differences between men and women exist at the most basic elements of human life. Can you imagine for a moment what would happen if a single male cell ever resided in a female body?

If women had just one male cell residing in their bodies, they would want sex twenty-four hours a day. (*Yes!!!*) They would sit reading on the toilet for hours. At the breakfast table, their face would be permanently blocked by the sports page. Women would finally see what it's like to take the trash out in rain, sleet, and snow. They'd have to admit fault for any argument and apologize for just about everything except breathing. Upon arriving home from a long day at the office, they would take one look at the house and ask stupid questions like, "What have you been doing all day long?" Insensitive and rash, women would communicate in grunts, shrugs, sign language, and mental telepathy. They'd be completely clueless on how to change a diaper. Pretending to be eighteen years old again, women would transform into weekend warriors twisting ankles, pulling hamstrings, complaining about their backs, and only visiting the doctor if involved in a major auto accident. Worst of all, women would control the remote! Aaaahhhhh!

If you want a really scary thought regarding this Franken-stein-like genetic reengineering, what if a single female cell were planted inside the bodies of men? Every two-car garage in every neighborhood throughout America would become a giant closet! Ice-skating, softball, and synchronized swimming would be the only sports on television. Men would change eight times before finally wearing the first outfit they tried on. They'd watch "chick flicks." When Mom is away, the kids would be clean, well-groomed, and fed from the four basic food groups instead of eating Happy Meals and Froot Loops all weekend long. Guys would go to the bathroom in twos, threes, or small groups of one hundred.

Burping and passing gas in public would be history. Men would start asking no-win questions like, "Do you like my outfit?" "How do you like my haircut?" and "Do I look fat?" Males would no longer be macho, strong, competitive, analytical, opinionated types, but instead they'd be sensitive, caring, nurturing, and intuitively smart. With that single female cell, men would cry watching soaps and get angry at those other dumb men on *Oprah.* They'd also discover the joys of PMS— *what vengeance!* Unable to handle the rigors of childbirth, all men would go straight for an epidural as they smoke cigars and play poker while waiting for a C-section. Most important, the toilet seat would always be put back down.

Thank God there's no X in Y chromosomes and no Y in X chromosomes. What a scary mix!

Common Ground

Except for books about Volkswagen repair, there are more books than ever in the market today about the differences between men and women. I still have trouble remembering the difference between the two symbols on bathroom doors. After reading several books on relationships from reputed authorities who purported to solve the male mystique and the female phenomenon, I now know why so many people escape into fiction.

Understand what makes a woman tick and you'll win her heart forever. That guy is really in for a blast when he realizes the soft, sexy ticktock of his woman is nothing but a time bomb ready to go off in his face.

Making meaningful sense out of the mind and muscle of your man. Researchers have recently confirmed that, like dinosaurs, the larger the muscles in a man, the smaller the brain. If the brontosaurus had a walnut-size brain, what would be the proportional size of a man's brain? A poppy seed? Pollen?

If you've been married for fifteen or twenty years or longer, you probably stopped trying to figure out your spouse long ago, but for those younger whippersnappers reading this who think they've got a fix on the opposite sex, give it a rest. Stop trying so hard.

The greatest challenge in your marriage is not to figure out why your husband thinks and acts the way *he* does or why your wife thinks and acts the way *she* does, but to figure out what makes your marriage work.

It's common knowledge that men are known to be logical, competitive, analytical, assertive, rational, and productive. In a similar way, women are known to be intuitive, feeling, accepting, loving, nurturing, compassionate, and synthetic. Though many of these traits are influenced by cultural norms and stereotypes, none of these traits are mutually exclusive when it comes to the opposite sex. All of these are qualities and traits that make a marriage work.

Most people get married based upon the qualities and traits they see and like in their future spouse. They downplay the qualities they don't like and elevate the qualities they do like. All of this is done to establish the common ground on which to build the marriage. After a few years of marriage, though, it's tempting to try to figure out and fix the qualities in our mates that we don't especially like. And of course, such behavior leads to extremes.

Instead of trying to figure out aspects of your spouse that you may never truly understand, why not celebrate character qualities and traits in your spouse that you appreciate and do understand? What is something unique that your spouse brings to your marriage? What qualities does he or she have that strengthen your marriage? What is one quality of your spouse that you would like more of yourself? Is your spouse creative or industrious? Caring or disciplined? Thoughtful or enthusiastic? Resourceful or playful? Witty or wise? What does your spouse bring to your marriage that makes it work?

Even if you and your spouse are dealing with ongoing conflict, as hard as it sounds, focus on your spouse's strengths, not on weaknesses. Common ground is built upon the shared strengths in each marriage. Why? So there will be a firm foundation to support the areas of weakness in each person's life. Focus on your spouse's weaknesses, and you will be forever disappointed.

Find a character quality you like about your husband or wife today. Now go tell 'em and explain why. It's probably worth going ape over.

I Know Exactly Where I'm Going

12

Why does it take 500 million sperm to fertilize one egg?
Because they won't stop to ask directions.

Put a guy behind the wheel of a car and he will drive you insane. How is it that there are millions of men who love to restore cars, spending whole days with their heads underneath the hood, washing and waxing their cars cleaner than they do their own kids, attending drag and stock car races so they can see their favorite driver blown to smithereens, and passing their Matchbox derby car collection down to the next generation, but when it comes to operating a vehicle on the road, they get lost quicker than they lose their wallet or watch?

Now we know why Motel 6 leaves the light on.

Let's say it's Saturday morning and your husband comes up with the great idea to take you and the kids fishing for the day. Sounds fun. The lake is only an hour away. You'll be able to relax under a tree and read a favorite book while your husband takes the kids fishing in a boat. So everybody gets their things together, a lunch is packed and then, *you get in the car.* That is your first and only mistake.

The first few minutes of your journey are fine. You back out of the driveway. Then your husband begins to navigate the car through town, which he knows fairly well, since he grew up here. He makes it to the freeway without a hitch and takes the interstate going due east. So far, you're happy, your husband's happy, your 2.5 kids in the back are happy. Everybody's happy. That is, until your husband gets cut off by an eighteen-wheeler carrying a load of cattle.

Enter road rage.

Suddenly, your husband becomes a vile, hideous beast.

"That idiot! I'll show him!"

Your husband steps on the gas. Your minivan lurches forward and zooms past all the cattle with bored expressions on their faces. As he passes the semi cab, your husband waves his left hand out the window and shouts to the trucker in bold, expressive sign language.

The trucker responds to your husband's physical vulgarities with a blast of his horn, which your kids think is cool, and they begin laughing.

"Quiet back there," your husband shouts. "I'm trying to drive!"

Your husband swerves over in front of the trucker and slows down to forty-five miles an hour, which causes the trucker to jam on his brakes. Your van almost gets rear-ended and you yell at your husband to calm down. The cattle in back aren't too happy about that manure, uh, maneuver either. They get into the fray by huddling together and coming up with a plan to moooooooon your husband on the next pass.

Your husband pumps his fist and shouts, "Ha! That'll show him! That's the last time he cuts me off!"

You look over at your husband and he's hunched over the wheel with a devious, sinister smile on his face. His forehead is perspiring, his cheeks are flushed, and he has that wild "do or die" look in his bloodshot eyes.

Now it's your turn to get angry.

"Would you calm down and start acting like an adult? If you want to kill yourself today, then fine! Just don't take me and the kids with you!"

"Me? I didn't start it—he did!"

In the backseat, a fight erupts between your son and daughter over whose turn it is to use the handheld *Annihilate Your World* video game.

"It's my turn to annihilate the world! Give me it!"

"No it's not! It's my turn to annihilate the world—you had your chance to use your thermoneutron missiles and you blew it. Let go before I annihilate you!"

You jump in before World War III erupts.

"Okay, both of you, that's enough!"

"Mom, Billy never shares with me. Make him share!"

"I'm not sharing with you, slugbreath."

That comment starts a ferocious scratching-kicking-slapping-hairpulling-punching-biting-screaming melee like you've never seen before. You glare at your husband and mutter something about modeling appropriate driving behavior. Unfortunately, you left your pepper spray back at home, but your husband finally comes to your aid with the one command that has sent chills down the back of every kid in a car since Henry Ford first used it on his children.

"DON'T MAKE ME STOP THIS CAR!"

Your husband has saved the world from annihilation, but suddenly you realize he missed the turnoff to the lake a mile back.

"I did not miss the turnoff."

And then, oh those fateful words that even Moses said to his wife thousands of years ago—

"I know exactly where I'm going."

If he had to, you know your husband couldn't find his way out of a paper bag. Gently, ever so subtly, you gingerly suggest that your husband turn around and go back to the exit that was marked, "Hey, you moron—your wife was right! The lake is this way!"

As expected, he will hear none of it and he proceeds to take the interchange that will soon put you into the next state.

"Why don't we just pull over to a gas station and ask for directions? What's wrong with asking directions?"

"Directions?" he shouts. "Directions! I don't need no stinking directions. I already told you, *I know exactly where I'm going!* Did Columbus ever pull into a gas station and ask for directions? Did Lewis and Clark ever ask for directions? Did the captain of the *Titanic* ever ask for directions? How dare you challenge my manhood! I have magnetic north in my blood. I am like a Global Positioning System. A bloodhound. A Cracker Jack compass. I have complete mastery over my surroundings. I don't need to ask for directions. *I know exactly where I'm going!"*

"Dad! That sign says, 'Welcome to South Dakota.' I didn't know the lake was in another state."

"Uh, well, that's right, son. There are lots of lakes in South Dakota."

This brings us to another point of interest in our little excursion: Men will take driving directions, input, or advice from their children, but never their wives.

Four hours later, you are all hopelessly lost as you pull into a greasy roadside diner run by cockroaches and large black flies. Your one unplanned stop was Mount Rushmore, but it was foggy, and you couldn't see our nation's strongest leaders pointing your husband in the right direction.

Common Ground

I'm convinced that men are the major cause of traffic jams because they often don't have a clue about where they're going. Guys have a terminal case of driving dyslexia. Most people don't know it, but AAA (the American Automobile Association) began as a discreet service to help men who were lost on the road, but could never admit it to their wives. To be fair, I'm also convinced that women are the leading cause of traffic accidents because they're trying to do their nails or put on makeup or curl their hair or write a note to a friend or pour juice into a bottle or talk on a cell phone or sip a latte while they drive.

Women will joke about men who find it extremely difficult to ask for directions and men have their jokes about women drivers, but the one thing that all marriages need is clear direction. No marriage can grow and develop without a clear sense of direction. Couples need to share a common vision for their lives in order to grow in the same direction for today and the years to come.

I was playing golf with a friend a while ago and we got to talking about our marriages. My friend Steve made a comment I'll never forget. He said, "Every one of the guys who was in my wedding party is now divorced."

A whole wedding party? *Divorced*?

Steve's comment made me wonder what the relationship was between divorce and losing direction in marriage. Nowadays, it's not too hard for couples to get lost in marriage. I mentioned earlier in the book that all sorts of things can knock couples off common ground. Fights. Finances. Busyness. Expectations. Kids. In-laws. Health struggles. Work. Loss. Communication problems. Sex. Stress. You name it—

It's so easy to get wrapped up in the challenges and responsibilities of everyday living that if a couple aren't careful to make it a priority to get on common ground every day, they just might find themselves growing apart from each other. So how do you get on common ground every day? How can you be sure you and your husband are growing in the same direction?

The first and most important thing to do to get on common ground is to make it a priority to connect with each other every day about your day. Talk about your day with each other. Share your high points and low points. Talk about your latest project at work. Share what you did with your friends or the kids. If you and your spouse haven't seen each other for most of the day, make the effort to reconnect in the evening by talking about your day. Tell the kids to split and devote twenty minutes to each other and catch up on the day's events.

Next, find some time during the week to regularly touch base on the major areas of home life. If these areas are ignored or left unattended for very long, they soon drive couples to extremes. Talk about your schedule. Your finances. What's happening with the kids. Anything related to career moves. Responsibilities around the house. Whether you have a weekly scheduled meeting, go out for a casual cup of coffee, or spend a little time talking together in bed before going to sleep, make it happen to be sure you and your spouse are on common ground about these important areas of home life.

Talking about your day and home life is essential to staying connected, but what will really keep you connected to each other is deep, intimate conversation. This is the heart-to-heart conversation that's critical to growing a marriage in a healthy direction. Intimate conversation is where you share and listen to each other's dreams, hopes, fears, disappointments, desires, needs, and aspirations. This is when you're honest and vulnerable even when it hurts. This is where you give each other your undivided and complete attention by essentially saying, "You are the most important person in my day." It's where you let down the walls and show the real you.

Intimate conversation has to happen if two people want to grow in the same direction. This is where you find out what your spouse needs from you and what you need from your spouse. This is where you ask how you can support and pray for one another. This is where you share Scripture together to discover God's direction for your marriage. This is where you pray to God and ask Him to give you the strength to live unselfish lives devoted to Him and to each other. This is where you also ask Him for the courage and vision and direction to make your marriage a truly great marriage.

There is no substitute for deep, intimate conversation to get your marriage on common ground. As you share your lives together by honestly opening your heart, you will grow in the same direction as you both learn how to serve one another in love.

And that's exactly where you want to be going.

I'm Not the Problem . . . You Are!

13

Marriages are made in heaven.
Then again, so are thunder and lightning.

I just returned from a relaxing four-day surf trip to Baja California. It's become an annual trip with ten of us guys who like surfing, fish tacos, yukking it up, the hot sun, campfires at night, motorcycle riding, a few days of no honey-dos, and gross guy talk. No, I'm not going to tell you what we talked about. I swore a blood oath.

It's the type of trip where nobody tells you what to do. You eat when you want to eat. You surf when you want to surf. You take a siesta whenever you want to take a siesta. About the only responsibility we guys have on this trip is showing up to go and cleaning up to go home. That's the way we guys like it.

Simple. Clean. Uncomplicated. No extremes.

No women.

This year we camped on the bluffs above a popular surfing spot called K38. Known for its clean, right-breaking waves off a rocky point, K38 can handle large south swells generated by huge tropical storms thousands of miles out in the Pacific Ocean. This year, we just happened to hit one of those storms just right.

El Niño spanked us like wicked stepchildren—the surf was enormous!

I like to surf, but I don't like to die. Give me solid six- to eight-foot waves and I'm a happy camper. But give me waves that are consistently double-overhead with the set waves maxing out at fifteen feet, and the outside of my wet suit isn't going to be the only thing that's wet. Catching one of these monsters is like jumping onto a moving locomotive. More than a few times, I got pile-driven and hammered like a piece of sushi on a machine press.

For those of you reading this who don't surf and don't understand what it's like to get the full-rinse Maytag thrash cycle when you attempt to dive under a ten-foot oncoming wall of water, think of the movie *Titanic*. Remember when the ship was sinking and the captain walks to the helm of the ship to go down with it? Remember when the glass breaks and that humongous wall of water takes him out like a tsunami?

Now just imagine taking a beating like that over and over during an eight-wave set. Thankfully, I wasn't the only one getting thumped. Armed with binoculars at our campsite on the bluffs, all of us took turns watching and laughing at one another getting pummeled in the head-crushing surf. Kudos to Craig, Todd, Phil, and Glen for rhino-charging hard and catching the biggest waves. The rest of us were happy to make it out of the water and out of Mexico with our lives.

Every day of the trip, the surf grew bigger and bigger. High tide. Low tide. The waves kept pounding in massive sets. Relentless. Just when I thought I was far enough outside the break, an even larger set of waves began looming over the horizon. As I paddled over the surging lip of the first few waves, the offshore winds blew billowing, salty showers of spray down the thick, curled backs of each wave.

On Saturday, we ventured down the road to check out another surf spot called K55, which was only seventeen kilometers down the road. It's a good thing all the Northern Baja surf spots stop well before K99. Any numbers three digits or higher and surfers start having problems.

As we stood in the hot sun on the cliffs above K55, the surf was absolutely "Macking," as in annihilation by a Mack truck. To the north, huge waves were peeling off the far point in a way we'd never seen that point break. In front of us, a foamy mass of white water led to deep blue water where the waves were breaking a half mile offshore. To the south, there was a Godzilla-like peak pounding the shorebreak.

We eagerly pulled on our wet suits and scaled down a steep, narrow, twisting trail to the sandy beach below. I was the first one down and the view from the beach was certainly different. The surf in front of me looked like a constantly surging white water rapid. Wall after wall after wall of whitewash charged toward the beach like the landing forces at Normandy. Out in the far distance, the waves now seemed to be at least a mile offshore. There was a slight channel a hundred yards up the beach, but that section of surf was getting hammered just as hard.

Since I was the first on the beach, I was also the first in the water.

Call me a wet guinea pig.

I paddled out thirty, maybe forty yards and got howitzered back to the beach. After one particularly brutal thrashing, I said, "Okay, that's enough. I have nothing to prove."

Assessing my brief foray into the merciless surf, the eight other guys held a board meeting right there on the sand. They conferred with one another over the likelihood of making the paddle out. They all agreed to throw in the beach towel and head back to K38, which at least had a channel to paddle out in.

Good decision.

Common Ground

Problems in marriage are often a matter of perspective. When we were standing on the cliffs checking out the surf, there didn't appear to be any problem paddling out. I knew the waves were big, but we'd been paddling out in large surf for the past two days. Then, when I stood on the beach seventy-five feet below the cliffs, you could say my perspective changed. Just a bit.

From the cliffs, I saw the potential for riding exhilarating waves.

From the beach, I encountered problem after problem of pounding surf.

I got worked.

And humbled.

You and your spouse are paddling the same board as other people reading this book. You all experience conflicts in your marriage. Personality conflicts. Job conflicts. Financial conflicts. Role conflicts. Communication conflicts. Health problems. Identity and self-esteem problems. Spiritual problems. Sexual problems. Trouble raising the kids or dealing with in-laws. Problems, problems, problems. It's a way of life on Planet Earth.

All of these problems can knock you off common ground. When faced with struggles in your marriage, it's easy for the common values, needs, interests, likes, and dislikes you both share to get pushed aside by the sheer force of the problem. Like monster surf, problems can push you and your spouse off the common ground that strengthens and unites your marriage.

Women are always right and men are never wrong because when conflicts arise, both sexes dig in deeper than Saharan sand dunes by refusing to look at the problem from the other perspective. That's extreme. It's part of our human nature. Women want to be right and men don't want to be wrong. Vice versa—it's all the same thing.

Just as there are tropical storms far off in the Pacific during certain seasons of the year, there are also stormy seasons in marriage. Every marriage needs to be equipped to handle these seasons. One of the most useful ways to make it through the definite disagreements, problems, and arguments that are a part of every marriage is to be willing to look at these conflicts from your spouse's perspective.

During a fight, couples get dug into their defensive positions and refuse to explore what the other person may be thinking or feeling about the conflict.

One person is on the cliff.

The other is on the beach.

Your view of the problem is a matter of your perspective.

There's always another perspective.

You married another perspective.

No fight or argument happens in a vacuum. We are always acting and responding to each other based on our perception of what we say and do toward one another. We alone are responsible for our feelings and our reactions. Our spouses do not cause us to feel or react the way we do. Our reactions are based not on our spouse's behavior, but on how we think, feel, and ultimately choose to respond to that behavior.

Refusing to look at a conflict from another perspective creates extremes. The more we dig in, the more right we become.

Regardless of who's right and who's wrong in an argument, there won't be any resolution until each side yields to look at the other person's perspective.

If you want to show love to your wife, value her perspective. Ask for her opinion. As much as you may try to do the manly thing by trying to fix the problem, let her solve the problem with you. If she needs your help or advice, let her ask for it in her own time and way. Listen to her feelings and ask how you can better understand her perspective. Don't compare her to anyone else. Deal with the problem at hand; don't dig up the past. Be willing to say, "I was wrong. I'm sorry."

If you want to show love to your husband, respect his perspective. Find the positive points in his position. Don't try to verbalize his feelings for him. Tell him what you honestly feel about the problem. Don't try to change him, but seek to understand him first. Look at what other pressures or problems he may be dealing with in his life. Deal with the problem at hand; don't dig up the past. Be willing to say, "I was wrong. I'm sorry."

There is a lot to be gained from another perspective. Forgiveness. Peace. Understanding. Insight. Growth. And common ground. You can have common ground and still have different perspectives. No couple agrees on everything. (I hope.) What's important is agreeing about the right things in your marriage. Just make sure the view is clear from both vantage points. To resolve the problems in your marriage, the most important questions are not, "How can I get my husband or wife to see my perspective? How can he or she understand my position?" But, "Where do we stand on this issue? What is my spouse's perspective and what is my perspective?"

Two "I's" do not always equal one "we."

But one "we" can include two "I's."

Both perspectives can get you on common ground. Both perspectives can produce a great team. Both perspectives can get you through the stormy seasons that are a part of every marriage. Both perspectives can get you out of the heavy surf.

It's Been a Long Time—

14

At bedtime, the amorous husband prepares two aspirins and a glass of water for his wife. "What is this for?"
"For your headache, dear."
"But I don't have a headache."
"Good."

I honestly didn't know how I was going to start this chapter. Sex is the eight-hundred-pound gorilla in the bedroom many couples don't know how to talk about. *Yeah, King Kong scared me to death when I was a kid, but there's no way I'm going to let a lower primate stand between me and my wife.* Thankfully, my wife arrived home last night after dinner and a movie with her MOPS (Mothers of Preschoolers) group and gave me just the introduction I needed. For her important contribution, she will be rewarded with roses, diamonds, soft music, candlelight dinners, champagne kisses, endless nights of passionate romance, and, most important, child care upon request.

After Krista and her girlfriends had dinner, they walked into a large chain bookstore, where one of her friends asked in a loud voice, "Do you have *The Joy of Sex?*"

The woman at the front counter looked up and said, "Yes, but I'm not sure where it is. *Let me know when you find it.*" *The Joy of Sex.*

A lot of couples have figured out the sex part. That's easy. A matter of anatomical mechanics. But the joy part? I believe that the sex lives of many husbands and wives across America have drifted into the doldrums of routine and predictability because of bad information about how to attract the opposite sex. Allow me to illustrate—don't worry, I won't be drawing any diagrams.

Many husbands and wives think that buying a new perfume or cologne will make them more attractive and thus more sexually appealing to their spouses. Like hound dogs pursuing their quarry, this is where men and women have lost the scent of what it means to pursue the opposite sex.

Men's cologne and women's perfume are a part of the billion-dollar fragrance industry. The basic premise of the fragrance industry is not to sell fragrant products to mask personal body odor, but to increase a person's sex appeal. Perfumes and colognes should not be confused with deodorant.

Deodorant is the bio-combatant ammo used to neutralize repugnant body odor that motivates office coworkers, bystanders in line, and neighborhood dogs to wear gas masks whenever they are near a foul-smelling person. Perfumes and colognes are used to attract your spouse to you. Perfumes and colognes are believed to be a compelling agent for enhancing sex appeal, but nothing could be further from the truth.

How do we know fragrances are used to increase sex appeal? Flip through any men's or women's magazine and you'll find scores of gorgeous, scantily clad models in fragrance advertisements waiting for you, just begging you, to pull on that little scent strip, which, when activated, unleashes a noxious cloud powerful enough to drop a charging African bull elephant.

If you pull that scent strip, you will pass out. The manufacturers know this.

Left dazed and disoriented, after pulling yourself off the floor, you will never forget the smell of that product. In fact, if you go to a department store and pay insane amounts of money for what you now think is a love potion that will draw your spouse to you like a bee to a flower, you will eventually develop a resistance to the fragrance. When you put it on and grab your spouse in a passionate embrace, like the charging African bull elephant, your spouse will collapse in your arms and be unable to resist your *besos de amor* (love kisses).

But do these fragrances really work? Do Ralph Lauren, Elizabeth Taylor, Christian Dior, and Carl Lagerfeld really know how to whip up a whiff to arouse your spouse? Do fragrances increase your sex appeal? Will they stimulate your love life?

I think not.

A recent study was conducted by a university in the eastern United States and became the daily topic of Charles Osgood's clever radio program, *The Osgood File*. The study reported that traditional men's and women's fragrances, which were thought to arouse the libido, actually did nothing of the sort. The researchers combined a number of different smells, fragrances, and aromas to find out which smells men and women most often associated with sex. The results?

The smells men most often associate with sex are donuts, licorice, and pumpkin pie.

For women, cucumbers and Good-n-Plenty candy.

As you can imagine, this study has profound financial implications for the fragrance industry. By the next fashion season, you can expect all the major designers to pull their current wares off department store shelves, replacing them with a whole new line of enticing fragrances. You'll see exotic-sounding labels like *Cucumber Obsession* by Calvin Klein, Ralph Lauren's *Licorice Whip,* and Tommy Hilfilgerboogerdigger's *Spicy Pumpkin.* We know for sure that Elizabeth Taylor will have a whole line of donut-related fragrances: *White Diamond Dunkers, GIANT Twist, National Velvet Buttermilk Beauty,* and, for customers who really want to dab it on thick, *Used Donut Grease.*

Now it shouldn't be any surprise that donuts, licorice, and pumpkin pie are the smells that men most often associate with sex. All women know that the way to a man's heart is through his stomach. But I'll bet if the university did further research they'd discover that guys will associate the smells of *all foods* with sex. It doesn't matter if it's quesadillas, bratwurst, ribs, tofu, navy bean soup, or salsa hot enough to start a stampede, food and sex are intricately linked in the mysterious male psyche. I must confess that even though I don't do donuts, two of my favorite smells are licorice and pumpkin pie.

Now that we have dismantled the fragrance myth, we have to ask the next most compelling question: Will sprinkling Good-n-Plenty and smearing pumpkin pie all over your bed improve your love life? That's a direction I'm not sure I want to head, but I can say that as I have been working on this book, the FDA has approved the release of Viagra to the sexually starved public. The resulting media storm has been overwhelming.

Jokes have abounded in the newspapers and on late-night talk shows over this new wonder drug that has done far more for married couples than what cucumbers and donuts may ever hope to do. NASA scientists are already talking about replacing space shuttle rocket fuel with Viagra. It was also reported that teenagers who dropped Viagra pills down the gas tanks of their Volkswagen Beetles were breaking land speed records. But at eight bucks a pill, Viagra is going to face stiff competition from powdered donuts that sell for fifty cents each.

If junk food and Viagra don't jump-start your love life, you may want to head back to the same bookstore that Krista and her friends went to. There's a new book by Mark Poncy that describes male midlife sexuality called (get this) *Manopause*. It's at the top of my "must read" list. Right after I finish *The Joy of*—

Common Ground

If your love life has been as fragrant as old rose water lately, maybe it's because you and your spouse have lost the passion and romance of each other's scent. You have your own unique way of being romanced and sexually aroused. So does your spouse. Because of the different way God has wired your bodies, you and your spouse have a unique way of being attracted to one another. To keep your love life alive, your job is to figure out your spouse's scent.

Sex is one subject over which couples often knock themselves off common ground. Two major killers of a healthy sex life between couples are busyness and lack of communication about each other's sexual needs. If you and your spouse make love, sex, and romance priorities in your marriage, not only will you help protect yourselves from extramarital affairs, but more important, you will enjoy a greater intimacy and devotion to one another. So what can you do if it's been a long time?

Make It a Priority to Communicate. A good sex life happens in the context of a healthy marriage, and honest communication with your spouse is a cornerstone of this book. Honest communication is what helps you avoid extremes by getting you on common ground. If you want to have a healthy, growing sexual relationship with your spouse, you need to talk with each other about what it will take to achieve that goal.

As I noted in earlier chapters, every marriage goes through all sorts of changes. Some are good, some not so good. Your work schedule and number of commitments will affect your sex life. Stress at home and work will affect your sex life. Having children and raising children will affect your sex life. Having children walk in on you while you're trying to have a healthy sex life will affect your sex life. Every marriage goes through periods of testing and transition, all of which will affect the intimacy you share with your spouse.

Regardless of what life stage your marriage is in, communication is critical to getting what you want and need for a healthy sex life in your marriage. Talk about your needs. Describe together what a healthy sex life means for your marriage. Be willing to compromise and negotiate. Ask each other what turns you on and what turns you off. If you have been insensitive to your spouse in the past, say you're sorry and be willing to forgive your spouse for any hurt they might have caused you. Before you hop into bed or wherever your favorite place is for making whoopee, do your homework by first getting on common ground and figuring out how to be more sensitive to each other's sexual needs through honest communication.

Understand the Unique Differences between Men and Women. Despite what some guys think, Letterman or Leno is no substitute for foreplay. Guys, women are wired for emotional intimacy before physical intimacy. If you want her, you have to understand her scent. Women, it doesn't matter if it's Pic-n-Save, the beach, an elevator, your bedroom, or the backyard, guys are wired to do it just about anywhere. Any time. If you want him, you have to understand his scent.

There is the extreme, age-old battle between guys and women over sex and romance. Women cry, "I can't just turn it on. I haven't seen my husband all day and the moment we hop into bed, he attacks me like a raving lunatic. Whatever happened to romance for romance's sake?" To which guys will counter, "What's wrong with sex for sex's sake? Guys are responsible for the procreation of the human race. *We've got a job to do!*"

Nothing is going to change the way guys and women are wired, so let's simplify this whole process. Guys, if you want sex, you have to work at what attracts your wife. Women, if you want romance, you have to work at what attracts your husband. Both of you have committed yourselves before God, family and friends to love each other 'til death do you part, so if you both want a healthy sex life, you both gotta work. Whoever said marriage is easy?

Guys, if you sincerely pay attention to your wife's needs for intimate conversation, time alone together, kind and thoughtful words, help around the house, and a bit of creative romance, you will make your wife feel special and loved. And sex will follow. I'm not promising immediately that night, but it will follow.

Wife, if you're willing to be spontaneous and occasionally take the lead in your sex life, you will put a big smile on your husband's face. Though there are some guys who are as dull as a plain donut, there are a lot of guys who like spontaneity and a bit of pizzazz. Guys are wired for sight and speed. Whatever God gave you, use what you got! Here's an idea: My wife told about one woman who got her husband's secretary to take a long lunch so she could sneak into his office and maul him when he returned. I hope the guy didn't work in a cubicle.

Be a Giver. Sex is a wonderful gift designed by God to be enjoyed by husbands and wives who love one another. The goal is to give, not to get. If you both give, you'll both get what you need. Get it?

If you and your spouse make your best effort to freely give yourselves to one another in love, then you will enjoy a mutually fulfilling sexual relationship. The best place to start is with honest communication and understanding what your spouse's sexual needs are. God wrote the book on the joy of sex, and He's designed that joy to be maximized in marriage. He didn't design sex to be dull and predictable. He made it to be *Good-n-Plenty.*

I Can't Live Up to Your Expectations!

15

Some people are so determined to find blissful happiness that they overlook a lifetime of contentment.

body odor isn't a subject that's covered in too many marriage books.

It really should be.

Nobody ever talks about body odor in marriage books, but body odor in marriage is as real as the tasty smell of bacon and eggs in the morning.

When dating, most couples have absolutely no clue what the other person smells like. Men and women do just about anything to mask their true bodily scents. In reference to the fragrance industry mentioned in the last chapter, men and women go to all extremes in purchasing expensive perfumes and cologne to woo their lovers. What about all the sweet-smelling soaps, deodorants, shampoos, conditioners, bubble baths, and Christmas tree air fresheners hanging on rearview mirrors that people buy to mask body odor that could knock a garbage truck sideways?

Frankly, I think all those perfumes, colognes, and deodorants are quite deceptive. A man or woman should have complete knowledge about their prospective spouse's scent long before they ever say "I do."

Body odor matters.

Now that I think about it a bit more, I'm beginning to work up a sweat over this smelly subject. A frank discussion about body odor should happen long before two people ever get engaged. It should even be a mandatory session in premarital counseling.

Come to think of it, talking about body odor may even take two or three sessions. There's a lot of different directions you could go. You've got foot odor. Armpit odor. There's breath odor. And bathroom odor. Don't forget about workout odor or greasy hair odor or wake up in the morning odor.

Lots of odors. Lots of issues to work through there.

And those are only the odors you can smell.

Scientists from the University of Chicago have finally proved the existence in humans of something called "pheromones." These are odorless chemicals released by one person that affect the behavior of others. In studies that began thirty-nine years ago, scientists discovered that insects secreted odorless chemicals that could change or affect the behavior of other insects in the same species. For example, scientists discovered that female monkeys in heat secrete a pheromone that works like an aphrodisiac to male monkeys. Call it a wild kingdom Viagra.

Pheromones also proved a significant factor in how hamsters chose their mates, how male elephants developed dominant relationships (similar to men's sporting events), and when baby rats were weaned from their mothers (which also depended on whether or not the baby rats had sharp teeth).

This landmark study of human beings releasing odorless chemicals that affect the behavior of others broke through years of speculation and heated controversy about whether human pheromones existed at all. But the results of this study shouldn't really surprise us. Odorless chemicals secreted by husbands and wives have affected each other's behavior for years. These "marriage pheromones" are secreted depending upon the time, place, and mood of males and females. Let's examine a few of these marriage pheromones to better understand how husbands and wives relate to each other. After reading this, couples who are considering marriage may want to take a second whiff.

The "Honey, Are You Awake?" Pheromone. This pheromone stimulates chemical communication involving sexual activity between a husband and his wife, usually when the guy can't sleep. This odorless chemical is secreted via a guy's vomeronasal organ (located in the back of his nose) around eleven-thirty at night. The guy's wife, however, is fast asleep after an exhausting day with the kids, and she wants to make love about as much as she wants to scrub the inside of a trash can. Unbeknownst to her, the guy showers his sleeping wife with his odorless pheromone. When he goes to wake her, this pheromone will stimulate the slumbering passion within her, and she will eagerly respond to his late-night advances. Of course, we all know there isn't one ounce of truth to this, but it sounds good in theory.

The "You Should Really See a Doctor" Pheromone. Men don't handle pain very well and their wives know this. Guys like going to doctors about as much as they like getting their teeth pulled. They don't want to be accused of being whiners or wimps. So they'll put up with broken bones, torn ligaments, eviscerated organs—just about anything to avoid going to a doctor. Wives also know that their husbands don't want them nagging them to go to the doctor. That is why wives have an odorless pheromone that cues their husbands it's time to go to the doctor.

A guy will fight this pheromone at first. He knows it exists in his wife, but he will try to fight it off by claiming there's nothing that four dozen Advil a day won't cure. Eventually, this female pheromone will work as a mild anesthetic to numb her husband's mind into compliance. When the guy arrives home from the doctor, the lingering aftereffects of the pheromone will cause him to convince himself that going to the doctor was all his own idea.

The "I Had a Long, Hard Day" Pheromone. This is where male and female pheromones pit themselves against each other to get out of doing an undesirable task. In traditional homes, the husband will drag himself through the front door after a long day and spray his pheromone all over the house. He expects his wife to pick this up and serve him like he was royalty just because he had "a long, hard day." Unfortunately for this guy, his wife has also had "a long, hard day" and she already sprayed her pheromone all over the house *before he got home.* This action completely neutralizes the husband's pheromone and so he must serve her as royalty.

In two-income families, the real challenge in secreting the "long, hard day" pheromone is fighting the drive home traffic. Whoever arrives home first and establishes pheromone priority wins. Sometimes via cell phone, one spouse will try to digitally transmit their pheromones to the answering machine at home. The pheromone dispersion ratio isn't as strong as walking through each room of the home, but it establishes a preliminary presence. This cell phone pheromone technology has not been fully developed yet, but it has been proven effective with pagers.

Common Ground

The discovery of human pheromones suggests that chemistry does matter between a husband and a wife. Men and women get married because of good chemistry. They marry because they share common ground in what they enjoy in one another. They share similar interests, values, principles, goals, beliefs, dreams, and desires. They are attracted to one another physically, mentally, emotionally, and spiritually. The intoxicating experience of romantic euphoria and enchantment between some couples makes them feel that their marriage is destined to be a lifetime of love and excitement.

And then enters a small, unseen group of odorless chemicals called "expectations."

Every person enters marriage with expectations and every marriage is defined by a particular set of expectations. Certain expectations are inevitable and common to all marriages. Expectations of each person, to the best of their ability, to meet their spouse's physical, emotional, spiritual, and sexual needs. Expectations of a growing, intimate marriage. Expectations of happiness and contentment. Expectations of rest and relaxation. Expectations of fidelity, integrity, and honesty. Expectations of provision and raising a family. Expectations of resolving conflict. Expectations of support and nurture. These are positive expectations that serve as the essential framework for constructing a marriage that works. Every couple needs to identify realistic expectations and unrealistic expectations for their marriage because nothing will ruin a marriage quicker than the bad odorless pheromones of unrealistic expectations. They are like a razor's edge that cuts a spouse every time he or she doesn't measure up.

Hear me now: *If you want a happy marriage—a marriage on common ground—lower your expectations.*

Lowering your expectations from what you think or feel your spouse *should* provide for you is one of the most basic principles to having a healthy marriage. It's been said that unrealistic expectations are planned disappointments. How many people do you know who are constantly hurt, consistently disappointed, and consumed by their own unrealistically high expectations?

Unrealistic expectations are cancer to a marriage.

For whatever reason, if a husband or wife can never measure up, be enough, provide enough, or do enough to please the other spouse, there will come a day when the discouraged spouse wakes up and decides to do something the other spouse would never expect: *Sayonara! I'm tired of being made to feel like chop suey.*

Guys don't want high-maintenance wives that they can never please. You can do one thing that will make your husband happy: Be easy to please. If you are always looking forward to the next biggest house, the next expensive car, the next piece of jewelry, the next exotic vacation, the next day of health spa pampering, the next weekly bouquet of flowers, little gift surprises, love letters left on the pillow every night, et cetera, *ad nauseam,* pretty soon your guy is going to get sick of delivering the goods. No man can meet the deeper emotional needs of a woman with unrealistically high expectations who chooses to define herself by material possessions. It's impossible!

Likewise, women want men who will respect, encourage, and support them. Women have a hard time being expected to "submit" if their husbands are not willing to serve. Guys, you will have a better marriage if you willingly make the first move to serve your wife. If you want to make your wife happy, put her needs and interests ahead of your own. Don't make her live against a straight edge of unrealistic expectations about how the house should look every day and how the kids should all be in their places with bright, shiny faces. You are now living in a different era from when your mother related to your father. *Your wife is not your mother.* It's a shock for some guys, I know. Your wife needs to know that she and the kids come first before your career, your softball team, your golf game, the TV, and your commitments to community and church events.

How can you and your spouse get on common ground by developing healthy, realistic expectations for each other in your marriage?

1. Lower Your Expectations. If you aren't happy in your marriage, is it because your expectations are way too high? Your spouse can't *make* you be happy and filled with joy over your life. That's something that only God can give. If you're fighting bitterness or anger at your spouse, is it because he or she (or your marriage) hasn't measured up to what you expect him or her (or it) to be? What is the root of your unrealistic expectations? What hurt or loss have you experienced that causes you to place unrealistic pressure on your spouse?

2. Lower Your Expectations. When people are getting married, they do everything in the world to convince everyone else that they've finally found the person that's right for them. Then, when they aren't happy in their marriage and they want out, they do everything in the world to convince everyone else that they picked the person that *wasn't* right for them. That's a bit extreme. Why set yourself up with unrealistic expectations only to be let down? Lower your expectations and be pleasantly surprised.

3. Lower Your Expectations. Instead of always focusing on what your spouse isn't doing or isn't providing or how you wish they would change, why not take a personal inventory and see what needs changing in you first? It's always a lot easier to expect the other person to change first, especially when you have a laundry list of items they're not living up to.

Unrealistic high expectations are odorless, toxic chemicals to a marriage.

They are extremes that will sap the life out of the spouse who's expected to bear a weight no one can shoulder on their own. There's a verse in the Bible that says it best, "Carry each other's burdens, and in this way you will fulfill the law of Christ" (Galatians 6:2). The law of Christ is the law of unconditional love. God loves you unconditionally not for what you do or don't do, but for who you are. What a refreshing, fragrant way to love your spouse.

I'll Be Ready in a Minute!

16

If a man stands alone in the forest, and there are no women around to hear what he says, is he still WRONG?

Sad, but true, many important words in marriage have lost their value in today's fast-paced world of communication breakthroughs. Some of the most important words couples have been saying to each other for years are being diluted and dulled by endless repetition.

When you say to your husband, "I'll be ready in a minute," don't you know that he knows you're lying? For the Lord, one day may be like a thousand years and a thousand years like one day, but to your husband who's waiting to go out for the evening, your one minute is much longer than the Lord's millennium.

What about guys? When you shout from underneath the car, "I'm almost done," don't you know that your wife knows you're lying? There are car parts lying all over the front lawn like a demolition derby. She can see that. Your "almost done" is a flat-out lie because every woman knows that a man's work is never done.

Or what about when you tell your wife, "Don't worry about it"? One of a wife's main jobs in life is to worry. Are you going to strip her of that privilege? She is supposed to worry about how she looks, worry about how the kids do in school, worry about getting the right wedding gift, worry about whether the newlywed couple will like her wedding gift or take it back like the ungrateful couple in chapter 7, worry about your getting paid on time, worry about what she thinks other women think about her, worry about her parents *and* your parents, and worry about the pets (not to be confused with your parents). By telling your wife not to worry about whatever she's worrying about, you are inadvertently depriving your wife of her worrisome role as a woman. If your wife wants to worry, she'll worry. If you don't understand this, you are simply wasting your words.

Similarly, when your wife tells you, "Don't sweat the small stuff," it's obvious that she's from Venus and thinks you're from Uranus. It is your job to sweat the small stuff—you are a man! It is your job to perform and prove yourself. Sweating the small stuff, along with the equally nerve-racking "It's no big deal," shows how extreme the galaxy gap is between you and your wife.

It is your job to sweat when you hear the thrashing, tearing sound of power and telephone cables as you Roto-Till your front yard. It is your job to sweat when that tiny part that costs two hundred bucks slips between your fingers and falls down the drain. It is your job to sweat when your wife forgets to put oil in the engine like you asked her to a month ago. It is your job to sweat when your teenage son is accompanied to the front door of your house by a nice police officer. It is your job to sweat when you hear rumors of layoffs, nuclear escalation, threats of terrorism, and news on sports radio that your favorite player is being traded to the worst team in the league. Sweating is a man's job, and it's all big stuff!

"I'll call if I'm going to be late" is another set of words that has been thrown into clichédom by male and female offenders alike. The operative word here is *if.* In order to enter the house without getting hit in the head by a flying shoe, the offending spouse who already knows he or she is in trouble for being drastically late and not calling, must assert that he or she didn't *think* they'd be late.

Already on the defensive like Bruce Lee fending off a dozen Ninja warriors, the offending spouse will say, "I said I'd call if I was going to be late. I *thought* I'd make it home on time. I didn't *think* I'd be late! I would have called if I had *known* I was going to be late."

Here, the conditional use of the word *if* is confused by the troublesome *thinking* and *knowing*. Thinking and knowing are critical to one's own sense of time and spatial relationships. Offending spouses who don't call when they're going to be late can be recalibrated to achieve a proper sense of time and space, but it's expensive.

Common Ground

Many marriages suffer because of words and phrases that have lost their value and, as a result, have become barriers to good communication. If you want your words to have value so your spouse will understand you, you need to become a good communicator. Good communication is vital to a healthy and happy marriage. Good communication will help you stay on common ground to keep your marriage moving forward. And when you go to those inevitable extremes in the middle of a conflict, good communication will get you back on common ground.

This is where Abraham Lincoln comes in.

Everyone loves Abraham Lincoln because he was a man of integrity. A man who fought for freedom. A man of courage and principle in the face of opposition. Lincoln was a brilliant communicator known for such famous speeches as *The Gettysburg Address, General Lee Is a Dork,* and *How to Be a Loser and Still Become President.*

Speaking of losers, Lincoln was a total loser. He wasn't always a great communicator. Ever read about how many elections he lost? Failed businesses he had? And then he became President. Only in America. He probably stuttered like Porky Pig before getting his oratory act together.

If you want to improve your communication skills with your spouse, there is hope. Lincoln developed what he called his *Timeless Communication Principles.* Let's look at what Abe had to say about communication and how it can make a difference in your marriage.

1. If You Want to Communicate Effectively, You Must Have Something to Say. There isn't too much to argue about on this one. Lincoln was a simple man.

For guys, this means, "Have a point."

For women, this means, "Get to the point."

2. Learn to Speak and Write Clearly. This boils down to considering whom the message is intended for. Men, don't slur your words together when you're angry. Stay calm and speak clearly. Women, don't yell in a shrill voice. That shrill is capable of breaking wineglasses and eardrums. If you leave your spouse a note explaining where you are going and when you expect to return, do not write in unintelligible doctor's scribble. Use block letters. Type the note if necessary.

3. Be Credible. This is a biggy in our house. If I mention to Krista an area in the house that needs attention and there just so happens to be a family of rats in the sink gnawing on leftover lambchop bones due to the mountainous pile of dishes I have neglected to wash, then I'm going to hear about it. Don't tote up black marks against your spouse unless your own chores are done.

4. Use Stories, Analogies, and Imagery. A lot of marriage counselors and people who have written marriage books like to use "word pictures." Word pictures help couples express their feelings in extreme, blazing fashion. For example, a wife who feels hurt by her husband's unkind words may use this word picture: "I feel as though, for no good reason, you lashed me to a wooden stake, poured airplane fuel over my whole body, and then flicked Ohio Blue Tip matches at me until I ignited like a Space Shuttle liftoff. *That's how the venom of your scathing, hydrochloric acid words made me feel.*"

Or a husband who feels jilted by his tired wife who has spurned his sexual advances at eleven-thirty at night may say, "Here I am [dramatic pause] wanting to nurture and hold you like a blossoming spring flower and you REJECT me as if I were poison ivy or jumping cactus or an Australian stinging tree or a Venus flytrap. *That's how I really feel—and if you think that's bad, you should see what my inner child has smeared all over its crib!*"

These examples may be a little extreme, but hey, this is a book about extremes. Use stories, analogies, and imagery to explain to your spouse how you feel, but leave the Shakespearean theatrics to Broadway.

5. Use Humor. Wives, if you're trying to get your husband to do a simple chore that he's been promising to do for months, use humor, but be careful how you use it. Don't use jokes like "What do you call a woman who works as hard as a man? *Lazy.*" Your guy will not be impressed, and he will put off hanging that picture frame for another two months.

Men, do not use crude language or any joke referring to a woman's body. Your wife will think: *(a)* You're talking about her body. *(b)* You're talking about another woman's body. Your wife doesn't want to hear your unsolicited comments about either subject.

6. Ask Good Questions. Don't ask stupid questions like I always do. My personal favorite is "How did that door ding get there?" I've now learned that there is indeed a door ding demon and it is not my wife.

Guys, your wife will gladly respond when you sincerely ask her how her day went and how she felt about it. If you can be a husband who takes initiative and interest in your wife's day, your words will definitely have value to her. You may be the only link to the only decent adult conversation she's had all day long.

7. Know Your Audience. Sorry to shatter the illusion here, but your spouse isn't going to accept every word, thought, or idea you present as a brilliant discovery adding to the body of human knowledge. Like every audience, your spouse will critique, examine, and weigh what you have to say. In fact, your spouse may be bored of you talking about the same things over and over. Know what words and ideas turn your spouse on (I'm not talking about sex here!). Engage your spouse in conversation with topics and subjects that interest him.

8. Convince Your Spouse You Are a Friend Who Has His or Her Own Best Interest at Heart. This one may be tough. Tell your husband, "Dear, you want to let me go out for the evening with my girlfriends because you will have the blessed opportunity to bond with your children, the fruit of your loins. When I return, I will be your maiden of love."

If that doesn't work, say, "Listen, bucko, like it or lump it, I'm going out with the girls tonight. I want the kids in bed by eight—no later—and all of their 2,037 toys picked up. Do this or you ain't getting any when I get home!"

9. Consider the Consequences of Your Message. A communiqué like point 8 may not go over that well, especially if your spouse's "own best interest" detector has stayed on zero. Some possible consequences of your message: (1) You'll get home to find 4,689 toys scattered in and around the sheet-and-blanket fort that snakes through every room in your home. (2) It's 10:30 P.M., the kids are still up and have overdosed on the mini-Snickers they had for dinner. (3) Your husband has cloistered himself in the bedroom with a renewed interest in *Victory at Sea* World War II movies on the History Channel.

10. Improve Your Ability a Little Bit Every Day. You can improve your ability to communicate with your spouse by simply making the time to sit down and talk each day. You can make what you say more valuable to your husband or wife by using encouraging, upbuilding words. You can become a better communicator by becoming a better listener. You can learn how to watch the silent cues you give away in your body language. You can learn how to ask for clarification if you don't understand what your spouse is saying. You can learn how not to interrupt or make hasty judgments. You can learn how to affirm and pray for your spouse when he is going through a tough time.

All these ideas can help you and your spouse become better communicators. By improving your communication skills, both of you will get on common ground and be able to talk about the things that matter most to each other and your marriage. These communication skills are critical to peace in your marriage and peace in your home.

Put these into practice and you should be able to avert a few civil wars.

I Have Nothing to Wear

17

A woman only has two complaints:
nothing to wear and not enough closet space.

Thank God my wife has learned the consumer shopping language of Targét.

That's French for Target. The store with a dollar sign for a bull's-eye.

I'll take Targét any day over those other dangerous foreign consumer languages women know from birth. Nordstrom. Bloomingdale's. Saks Fifth Avenue. Needless Markups.

I've already spent thousands of dollars on a speech therapist to rid her of that snooty Brit accent she picked up after spending only an hour in Laura Ashley.

That's right, dear, say it again—*Tar-tar-ge—Targét!*

Spoken with a slight, upward tilt of the nose, the languages of these expensive department stores and any remotely related specialty boutiques turn guys into frenzied financial analysts. I don't care if your husband is a plumber, a baker, or a candlestick maker, if you start speaking in tongues to the tune of Ralph Lauren or Laura Ashley, your husband is a financial analyst.

Mention how much you spent shopping today and your husband will quote the exact balance in your checking and savings accounts. Yes, down to the last penny, the most recent withdrawal, the last cleared check, and the interest earned in the last twenty-four hours. During nonshopping hours, your husband may not be able to count the toes on his feet or perform simple addition problems like $89.99 + $10.00 = $99.99, but at the first mention of other foreign words like *sale, credit card, personalized shopping*, and *preferred customer*, he will be all over you like a CPA on April 14.

Despite my wife's resentment of me playing with an abacus in bed, her progress at losing that Laura Ashley accent is actually quite good. Though I met some resistance at first, I've been teaching her short phrases from the language of America's most important store: *Wal-Mart*.

I'm even thinking of erecting a bronze statue of Sam Walton in my front yard as a tribute to this great American. Sam Walton has done more for the American economy and the American home than the Chairman of the Federal Reserve and any marriage counselor combined. He has championed a husband's favorite words—

Dime store.

When *Forbes* named good ol' Sam the richest man in America, what was the humble response from this modest owner of the largest retail store in the world? "The next thing we knew all these reporters and photographers arrived, I guess to take pictures of me diving into a swimming pool of money they imagined I had, or to watch me light big fat cigars with hundred-dollar bills while the hootchy-kootchy girls danced by the lake." When asked why he drives a pickup truck, Sam responded, "What am I supposed to haul my dogs around in, a Rolls Royce?"

Now that's a language a guy can understand!

It would be a complete exaggeration to insinuate that all women are wired to shop at expensive stores. Even though this book is about extremes, a general statement like that would be *too* extreme. It would also be politically incorrect. It would also be quite stupid. It would also lead to more than a few pipe bombs shipped to my recently changed mailing address.

Some women are very defensive with their dollars. That's why their husbands are always asking their buddies if they can borrow a few bucks. When it comes to squeezing a penny, some women can make Abraham Lincoln's ears bleed. They will drive across town to save a few bucks on a meal deal. They will buy clothes through catalogs to avoid paying state sales tax. They endure the agony of paper cuts and exasperated customers behind them as they wade through mounds of coupons in the checkout line. They pay the family bills on time and even put up with husbands who pull into the driveway with big-screen TVs and say, "Relax! We don't have to pay a dime for six months." And after six months, that dime will be a fifty-dollar monthly payment for the next thirty-six months plus interest.

Yes, there are some women who are truly defensive with their dollars and if that's you, you deserve a shopping spree at Wal-Mart.

I'm grateful my wife is defensive with our dollars. She isn't the type that has Dom Pérignon tastes on a Bud Light budget. But the one thing she has in common with all women, whether they are Nordstrom neophytes, sanctified Saks saints, or frugal, fiscally responsible coupon queens, is that she has nothing to wear. Ever.

I have nothing to wear is the mantra of all women, young and old alike.

I knew this from personal experience way before I was ever married. You see, I grew up in a home with five sisters and one brother. My brother and I always had clothes to wear. Jeans and a T-shirt. No problem. My sisters? They never had anything to wear. I don't know how my dad ever got the family anywhere on time with six women changing their clothes at least ten times each before they all screamed in unison, *"I have nothing to wear—WE HAVE NOTHING TO WEAR!"*

When I got married, even though my bride now had her sister's wedding dress, she still claimed she had nothing to wear. (As a new husband, I found her dilemma quite interesting.) The same is true for most women, married or not.

Another of the extreme marital inequalities I have yet to comprehend is this: How is it that women get nine-tenths of all closet space in the master bedroom and men get the remaining tenth plus a military footlocker under the bed? What ever happened to equal rights? Fifty-fifty includes closet space! Why must a man spread his entire wardrobe throughout the rest of the house in places like dark basements, dingy attics, and—if he doesn't mind the fleas—the doghouse?

This is a gross injustice.

It is all based upon the questionable premise that a woman has nothing to wear.

When preparing to go out to dinner or a party with friends, what well-meaning husband hasn't tried to help pick something out for his depressed, fashion-challenged wife to wear?

Here, honey, try this outfit. You look pretty in this one.

Not that dirty rag. I HATE THAT OUTFIT!

Okay, well, how about this one?

I'm sick of that outfit. I wore that last time!

I know, here's the dress you've always liked.

That dress makes me look fat!

Fine. I'll be in the car. You have five minutes.

Common Ground

This deep-seated lamentation of having nothing to wear, I'm sure, goes all the way back to the Fall. Adam would have been fine running around in the buff if Eve hadn't complained about having nothing to wear. I'm sure one of the great mysteries in the Bible is whether fig leaves were clothes or accessories. And when God made Adam and Eve garments out of skin, how many outfits did she ask for? Did that include a closet?

Guys, if your wife is complaining about having nothing to wear, pay attention. Chances are she is speaking about a deeper need that you can't see. That need may be buried far deeper in her heart than all the dresses, sweaters, skirts, blouses, shoes, pants, and, yes, accessories piled in her closet. Your wife may be feeling insecure, tired, or plain old ugly. When she says there's nothing in her closet, it could be because she sincerely detests every speck of clothing she owns, but it could also be because she feels empty inside. Her closet could be a reflection of her heart.

At times like this, what your wife really needs is encouragement. Telling her she has a closet full of clothes won't help one bit. Think about it: Most guys don't have a clue about what their wives go through all day long. Moms at home are constantly picking up after Godzilla-like toddlers. They drive carpools of screaming kids who aren't afraid of the warning, "Don't make me stop this car." Moms have to shop to satisfy culinary tastes that range from Pez to filet mignon. They clean bathrooms for no minimum wage. Their lives are put in physical danger by trying to separate two scratching, smacking siblings. They endure the endorpho-hormonal roller-coaster ride of teenagers' emotions. And after mopping up dog vomit from the living room rug, it's not hard for any mom to feel battered and bruised from the joys of motherhood.

Encouragement is one commodity that all wives and moms need in healthy doses. When there's nothing for her to wear, your wife needs to know that she is beautiful to you no matter what. She needs you to build her up when she's down, just as you need her support when you're having a bad day. By encouraging your wife in words and deeds, you will be filling her with far more than any closet of clothes could ever do.

What happens when you encourage your wife? The first thing you give her is a wonderful gift called *hope*. Your encouragement reminds her that she is still the pretty bride you married. Your encouragement renews her perspective that not all days are bad days. Your encouragement reminds her of the tender and special qualities inside of her, especially when she sees nothing of value on the outside. All this gives a woman hope, and hope is what will keep your wife growing to be the special woman God has created her to be.

The second thing you give your wife when you encourage her is *confidence. Working woman* is a term that confuses a lot of people today. All women work, but not all women get paid for working. Regardless of whether your wife is a career mom or a career cardiac surgeon, all women want to approach what they do with confidence. Some women who are professional moms feel like second-class citizens because the only marketplace they're ever in is the grocery store.

Your job as a husband and father is to make your wife feel like a million bucks for the critical part she plays in your home and family. Express your appreciation for what she does. Send her flowers when she least expects it. Compliment her for the little things she does to make your home a special place to live. Your encouragement will remind her that you're on her team. Do this and watch her confidence grow.

Last, when you encourage your wife, you will be filling her with the *courage* to take on each and every day on purpose. Many women find little purpose and meaning in what they do because they don't have husbands encouraging them to be a person of significance. When you encourage your wife, you are reminding her of your love, support, and belief in her. That's something every person needs.

Encourage your wife today and give her hope, confidence, and courage.

Those are three qualities she can wear with style.

Of course, buying her a new outfit will certainly make her happy too.

P.S. No joke, my wife read this chapter last night and gave it a thumbs-up. Today, she just walked into the house with a bagful of new clothes she bought for herself at Target. What could I say? *That's what I call entrapment!*

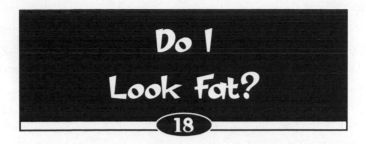

Do I Look Fat?

18

How am I supposed to answer that?

i was warned by a lot of guys not to write this chapter.

"Don't go there!" they cautioned me. "You are dealing with the most notorious no-win question every man fears. Take the Fifth Amendment!"

On and on they went, telling me that if I attempted to write about this weighty, heavy topic, I'd have to hire a personal security guard. I'd be attacked by hordes of Richard Simmons fans wanting to slice me into fish chum with their Deal-a-Meal cards, I'd spend years in court battling defamation lawsuits from Jenny Craig Weight Gain Centers and Roseanne Barr *Buns of Steel* videos, I'd have plastic surgeons lurking to liposuction my brain, and I'd finally be dragged into a dark alley by some angry husband whose wife forced him to read this book. As I lay beaten and bloodied amid the trash and rubble, this tormented husband would slowly proceed to choke me to death with his wife's own ThighMaster.

Okay, so I'm going to talk about what all women never stop talking about.

Believe it or not, this chapter is in defense of women's weight struggles. I do confess that I have read *Woman's Day* in the office of my wife's ob-gyn. Not exactly *Victoria's Secret,* but did I get some good recipe ideas. And that's what blew me away about that magazine—how could a woman read magazines like that and not gain weight? I've never seen so many ads for Duncan Hines, Toll House cookies, and Sara Lee desserts. The magazine I had in my hands must have contained a million grams of fat.

Not only do women have to resist the temptation to buy rich, buttery desserts advertised in magazines, it's nearly impossible for them not to compare themselves to all the gorgeous supermodels in those magazines.

What do sadistic, cruel grocers do every time a woman goes to the store to buy food for her family? They place all the *Cosmopolitan, Elle, Mademoiselle,* and *Women's Fitness* magazines right at the front of the checkout line. If a woman has innocently snatched a couple of cookies from the bag she's purchasing for her kids' lunches, what does she immediately begin to feel? *GUILT!* The sadistic grocer knows that if he can make a woman feel guilty for whatever's in the shopping cart that's not labeled fat-free, she will try to assuage her guilt by buying a magazine with "The New Grapefruit and Gummy Bear Diet" plastered all over the cover.

Our society places tremendous importance on beauty, health, and external appearances. No one feels this pressure more than women. Coupled with the unrealistic standards set by our society, guys have it really easy with the kid thing. If a woman wants to have children, she is volunteering her own body to take a beating. For nine months, her body will grow, stretch, and expand.

Just what a woman wants. Then, after the baby's born, she's left to restore what was destroyed by her former tenant.

Go ahead and say it—*It's just not fair!*

In some homes, women who are trying to watch their weight don't get much support from their husbands. A paunchy husband who's carrying around more than a few extra pounds may not care much about his wife's diet of birdseed and water, but it had better not get in the way of his butter brickle ice cream. His diet does nothing but frustrate her diet.

Gals, let's talk about guy fat. Some guys could not care less about what they weigh; they may even deny they have a weight problem. A guy in double-grab-of-flab denial reasons that he gets plenty of exercise in front of the TV during football, basketball, baseball, and monster truck rally seasons. Heck, if he's dashing back and forth from the kitchen, ripping open Pringle potato chip cans, squeezing the Cheese Wiz, inhaling slice after slice of pizza, clicking the remote, and maxing out the heart rate when the game goes into overtime, then he's getting in shape, right? It takes a lot of endurance to watch eight hours of sports on a Saturday and then to come back the next day and do it all over again. It takes discipline to develop a gut that would make the Michelin tire man jealous. A guy figures, "What comes on, comes off. No big deal."

A different but more damaging spin on this treadmill is the husband who is Mr. Muscle and Fitness Mega-Metabolic Fat-Burning Machine who goes to the gym six days a week and expects his wife to do the same. "Hey, honey, I met a woman who bench-presses 250 pounds and she's looking for a workout partner. I gave her our phone number and she's going to call you."

I can't completely bag on us guys without discussing the double standards that husbands have to deal with. Guys get totally painted into the proverbial corner of the weight room by wives who are hypersensitive about their weight. Women can go on and on talking with other women about their diets, losing weight, thunder thighs, feeling guilty for indulging in a pint of Haagen-Dazs ice cream, and how depressed they feel about their weight, but guys aren't allowed to enter the discussion. It is a "Females Only" conversation, but then what do wives do? They tease, poke, prod, and pinch their husbands' love handles! If a guy ever did that to his wife, he'd be castrated.

One obsession followed by both men and women who are metabolically challenged is the myth of fat-free food. Have you ever tasted anything that's labeled fat-free? Oh my gosh, the stuff tastes like recycled hamster sawdust. Anything labeled fat-free means "Tasteless." A recent study confirmed that all fat-free foods, it didn't matter if it was fat-free cookies, chips, crackers, dogfood, ice cream, yogurt, or other milk products, was scientifically proven to cause obesity in rats. In lab tests, mice actually chose to eat d-CON poison before anything labeled fat-free.

If you think that is bad, the U.S. government has just entered the battle of the bulge by dropping the obesity standards for men, women, and children all across America. Just yesterday, based on the new governmental guidelines, thirty million Americans woke up and discovered they went from fit to fat. The National Institutes of Health uses a measurement called the Body Mass Index, or BMI, to determine if you are overweight. Body Mass Index works like this: If you can breathe, you're fat.

It is known that Americans are the largest of all people on Planet Earth, but lowering the threshold for what constitutes chubbiness has sent millions of Americans into a depressing tailspin of diet defeatism. Shareholders of Ben & Jerry's gourmet ice cream are licking their just desserts, though. Ever since the new weight standard was reported, there's been a tenfold increase in the sales of Ben & Jerry's chunky monkey. And who is the secret major shareholder of Ben & Jerry's ice cream? You got it—the National Institutes of Health!

Some men and women forgo dieting all together by heading straight to their plastic surgeon. These secret little operations may be good for short-term cosmetic changes, but I certainly don't recommend them. How do you know whether a plastic surgeon has ever come dangerously close to major organs with those industrial-strength cellulite suckers? *Shut off the pump!! I think I've got a gall bladder!*

The single most agonizing question a woman can ask her husband is this: "Do I look fat?" Wife, don't do this to your husband. You are putting him in a double-bind, no-win situation. If you think it's not fair what pregnancy can do to your body, it's also not fair for a guy to have to respond to that question.

Conversations about fat usually begin when a husband and wife are standing in the bathroom in their underwear as they get ready for bed. Show me a wife who hasn't stood in front of the mirror and groaned, "I can't stand my body. Look at my rear—it is SO FAT!"

What is a guy supposed to say?

A wise husband will silently stand there brushing his teeth with his mouth so full of bluish-green foam he can't possibly enter this dangerous discussion.

"Look at my hips! They are SO LARGE!"

Knowing exactly where this discussion is heading, a wise husband will quickly move from toothpaste to flossing where nothing he says will be intelligible because of the floss and fingers in his mouth.

"Look at my whole body. It is SO HUGE!"

From flossing to mouthwash, the wise husband will do anything to avoid getting trapped in this dead-men-tell-no-fat-tales folly. Even though it is producing second-degree burns in his mouth and throat, a guy will repeatedly gargle with Listerine to keep his mouth from causing even more grievous physical damage to his body.

No matter how depressed you are about your body, do not put your husband in the crosshairs of this immortal question, *"DO I LOOK FAT?"*

Your husband knows that if he says, "No, you're not fat," then you will scream, *"Liar!"* and beat him into bloody tomato pulp. Guys, on this one issue, "no" means you're lying. All women think this. Don't mess up here—this is one of those times when women are always right. What she really wants and needs to hear is, "I love you just the way you are."

Say that, if you dare, but only that.

Common Ground

Weight is a sensitive issue for some couples, but not all couples. There are plenty of marriages where both husband and wife are overweight and the couple have a strong, healthy marriage. There may be other issues they need to deal with, but if both spouses accept each other the way they are, then there's no real weight problem. Despite all the beauty and glamour we see in magazines, on television commercials, and in movies, physical fitness is no measure for a healthy marriage. A healthy marriage is characterized by how husbands and wives honor and respect one another regardless of physical appearances. There is a great verse in the Bible that says, "Man looks at the outward appearance, but the LORD looks at the heart" (1 Samuel 16:7).

Here are two questions to consider: Whose standards do you use to define beauty and attraction in your marriage? Do you judge your spouse based on outward appearance or by what's in his or her heart?

Physical attraction is an important part of marriage, and we'd be foolish to pretend it isn't. But there's much more to marriage than physical attraction. My wife has friends who say without a doubt that they would prefer to be married to a less attractive guy who helps around the house than to be married to a handsome stud who's a dud and does nothing. Inner character, what's in your heart, is more important than physical appearance.

At the same time, don't underestimate the importance of good health and taking care of yourself. Serious health problems often start as small health problems. If you are out of shape and you're not taking care of yourself, you are more prone to sickness and disease. Health problems cause strain not only in your marriage, but in the longevity and quality of your life as well. Both you and your spouse need to be sure to take care of your health.

Whatever you look like and however you feel about your body, use what you've got to be attractive to your spouse, but more important, work on being a person of the heart. The qualities of goodness, kindness, gentleness, faithfulness, compassion, joy, understanding, and love are what makes a person truly attractive. Those are the qualities that help couples get on common ground and stay there. Those are the qualities worth investing in far more than a health club membership. These qualities of the heart are free *and* fat-free.

Love Handles

19

The great question . . . which I have
not been able to answer . . . is
"What does a woman want?"
—Freud

It's hard when jocks get old. No, I'm not talking about that disgusting piece of male underwear that was used as a slingshot by Saddam Hussein to launch SCUZ missiles during the Gulf War. I'm talking about guys who hate growing old. As the hairline gets thinner and the waistline gets wider, many guys enter into a physical and emotional syndrome similar to PMS.

Though loath to admit it exists, guys have kept it a national secret, almost a blood oath by reversing the letters. By doing this, they hope to avoid the same ridicule, scorn, and shame they have heaped for years on women with all their dumb PMS jokes. SMP, or Sure Misses Puberty, is a verifiable medical condition that can be diagnosed by any wife with a keen eye.

SMP is a regressive syndrome in which guys look back to the days of their youth when they were gaining body hair instead of losing it, increasing muscle mass instead of just putting on weight, improving in physical agility instead of buying infomercial exercise equipment that collects dust in the garage, and enjoying the thrill of athletic victories instead of blowing out their ACLs (that spaghetti-like knee ligament that scorns age, gravity, and egos that need humbling).

From an emotional standpoint, SMP is a longing for yesteryear when young guys had six-packs for stomachs and baseballs for biceps. During their developing adolescent years, guys had everything to look forward to. Strong physiques. Dating. Getting a driver's license. Getting a fast, hot car. Being a big stud on campus. They were growing into *men* and attracting the attention of *women*.

Now, these same guys are sagging into frumpy middle-age men who drive beige sedans, attracting only the attention of funeral package sellers. SMP causes guys to become moody, irritable, and irrational, especially when their daughters bring home studly, musclebound boyfriends who drive hot wheels.

The first stages of SMP are noticeable when guys sit in front of the TV set during the NBA finals or other sporting events and make delusions-of-grandeur comments like, "Look at Michael Jordan there. I tell you, if I woulda kept playing basketball, I coulda been like Michael Jordan. Tiger Woods? If I woulda picked up a golf club when I was three, I'd be wearing Nike every day. Hey, Gloria, the kids down the street would wanna be just like me. They'd see my commercials and say, *'I AM Vic Slobowski!'*"

The second sign of SMP occurs when a guy gets a phone call on Friday evening from a friend who needs to find a replacement player for tomorrow's game. Evidently, your friend says, the other guy's wife wouldn't let him out of the house until he finished some book about women always being right. Even though your husband hasn't touched a basketball in three years and the only cardiovascular exercise he's had is cleaning his bellybutton lint, he ignores you and waves you off as you shake your head and mouth very clearly, "NO, DON'T DO IT."

In his clearest, most confident-sounding voice, he says, "Sounds great—can't wait." That's your signal to have ice packs, Ace bandages, and an orthopedic trauma team prepared to do surgery on your kitchen table when he staggers through the door moaning like a mortally wounded moose.

No anesthesia.

You warned him.

You get the first cut.

The third and most obvious sign of SMP is when your husband begins to make egregious claims to athletic superiority that you and the rest of the family highly suspect he never had. It all starts one morning around the breakfast table when he's reading the Saturday sports page. Your ten-year-old son makes a comment about a local decathlon and your husband perks up from behind his paper.

"Hey, son, did you know that your father was once a decathlete?"

"Gee, Dad, you never told me about that. I thought you said you received the Tweezer Trophy for riding the pine for an entire season."

"Well, that was when I was a senior in high school, son. I went on to become an outstanding college decathlete. In fact, I even considered trying out for the Olympic track team."

Amazed at what your ears are hearing, you decide to enter this fascinating discussion of athletic achievement.

"That's funny, dear, you never told me about being a decathlete either."

"Well, it was before we met, honey. It's when I was in junior college."

"What was your favorite event, Dad?"

"Now that's a tough one—I really liked that flying feeling I got when pole-vaulting, and I probably could've been a whole lot better at the javelin if people had stayed outta my way, but I think I'd have to say my favorite event was the hammer throw. I loved throwing that ball and chain away."

"Is that where you learned to throw golf clubs, Dad?"

"Kinda sorta."

"Why don't you tell us about all the events you won before *I* take up the javelin, dear?"

"Well, let's see. There was the Tuskaloosa Open Invitational. Won that one while the tornado sirens were blaring. Set a record in the shot put that day. My shot put got sucked up into some tornado and nailed a lady's cow three miles down the road. Woulda been a national record if I hadn't killed the beast. Then, there was the Toadsuck, Arkansas, state meet. It was hailing the size of softballs that day, so none of the other teams showed. I won by forfeiture, but hey, a win is still a win. Then, there was the Annual Alumni Decathlon—oh, there's too many to remember, you'll have to ask Grandma. She's got all my old medals."

"Honey, your mother has been dead for five years now. We never found any medals when we went through her things."

"Is that so? Maybe it was ribbons they gave us. Those things don't last."

Once dementia like this has set in, the final sign of SMP is seen when your husband takes his shirt off before going to bed and you make a teasing comment about his cute little love handles. Of course, those love handles may be the circumference of an earthmover inner tube, but you know how irritated he gets when you finger his flab.

His first defense is to suck in enough air to inflate a hot-air balloon, which will reduce the size of his gut for about three seconds. Next, he'll flex his biceps to distract your eyes upward. The only significant change you notice, though, is how hairy his armpits have gotten. Since this doesn't produce the dignity and respect he so badly needs, he'll put words in your mouth as he projects his insecurities like an adolescent, a telltale sign of full-blown SMP syndrome.

"FAT? Who you calling fat? This stuff is stored muscle."

Your husband will go to bed in a huff as you giggle and poke at his love handles under the sheets.

"That's not funny! Keep your hands to yourself!"

The next morning, your chubby hubby drives downtown and joins an expensive health club, where he begins working out with a personalized trainer with no neck by the name of Dirk. The first test Dirk gives your husband is a body-fat test, which determines how many boxes of Famous Amos cookies your husband puts away each week. Next, Dirk shows your husband how to use the club's fitness equipment. This scares you because you know that Dirk doesn't know what your husband is like when he gets around heavy machinery.

After learning about reps, maxing out, and the health club mantra of re-racking weights, Dirk takes your husband over to the high-speed treadmill. Set on Level 2, your husband walks at an easy gait until he inadvertently hits Level 10, which launches him like a cruise missile into a women's aerobics class. After Dirk pulls your husband from the tangled mess of screaming, cursing bodies, he concludes that your husband's real problem is a lack of spandex. Formfitting clothing reduces wind resistance and should your husband ever hit Level 10 again, the spandex bodysuit recommended by Dirk will send him flying past the aerobics class and into the club swimming pool. There, the lifeguards will have an easy rescue. All they'll have to do is grab his love handles.

Common Ground

Guys get touchy about their love handles. A lot of guys undergo liposuction to get rid of their love handles, and I've actually thought about this. In fact, I was almost ready to call one of those cottage cheese doctors until I read an FBI report that states there's a strong correlation between liposuction machines and missing persons. I don't know about you, but I'd rather donate my body to science than to a vacuum cleaner.

We can joke about SMP, but herein lies a nugget of truth: Many guys long for the simpler days of sandlot baseball and leather gloves. That's not to say they don't like being husbands and fathers, but they do need a way to unwind. Sports provide the excitement and escape many guys need to balance the competition and pressure they face at work. Whether they're actively participating in sports or simply following their favorite team, sports give guys a needed outlet for the things that stress them out. This is where husbands and wives need to understand the importance of leisure time spent alone and leisure time spent together. A guy may want to watch a ball game alone or with some friends, but that doesn't mean he doesn't want to be with his wife.

Yes, some guys go to extremes with their favorite teams. These are the same guys who have made a national religion out of football, baseball, basketball, ice hockey, and synchronized swimming. But not all guys wear their team's face paint to bed. Some just wear it to work.

If your guy goes to extremes as a pro sports fanatic, allow him to indulge his fantasies. (As much as you can take, of course.) When he stands in front of the mirror, his love handles will remind him that his chest is sliding to his waist and that, with an intimidating stature of 5'9", he stands not-so-tall among the vertically challenged. This revelation will yank him from the clouds where he hovers near the basketball rim high above the arena floor back to the cold linoleum of everyday living.

If you yourself are a sports fanatic husband, it might be a good idea to remember that you've got a team of your own that is far more valuable than a professional sports franchise. Your sports widow isn't your agent or manager or concession stand server. Your kids aren't your bat boys or ball girls. You have a wife and children who need to know they come before the Yankees and Celts, the Dodgers and Bulls, the Rockets and Kings, the Forty Niners and Cowboys, and all the rest. That is sports sacrilege to the Sunday faithful, I know, but grab hold of this love handle—

The most important competition you and your spouse face is not what's on TV, but in winning the game of life together. To win in life and in marriage, you both need to be on common ground with how you prioritize your leisure time. If you can get a handle on spending time together doing something you both enjoy, you will see your love and affection for each other grow. Going for walks together, playing tennis, hiking, sailing, jogging, golfing, or going to an athletic event together can enhance your relationship in all sorts of positive ways. Recreation is designed by God to re-create our lives and rejuvenate our spirits. What better way to do this than with your spouse?

Make sure that being together tops your list when it comes to leisure time. Then, once that's covered, if your husband wants to go to a ball game or join a softball league, let him. If your wife wants to get out to enjoy something she loves to do, don't protest just because there isn't a game on. Sports may be your passion, but people are more important than sports. God has designed husbands and wives to run the race together for a lifetime. Put your spouse and family before sports and you'll have more love than you can handle.

Gimme Five Bucks

20

A lady asked her wealthy friend,
"What was your husband before he married you?"
"He used to be a billionaire,
but I made him a millionaire."

how is it that a married couple can mutually agree to spend hundreds of dollars on clothes, thousands of dollars on cars, hundreds of thousands of dollars on homes, and millions of dollars on college education loans, but the worst financial fights in marriage are always over five bucks?

- Gimme five bucks—I wanna hit a bucket of balls.

- Gimme five bucks—*You go get your own five bucks.*

- Gimme five bucks—I need to buy a Happy Meal at Mickey D's.

- Gimme five bucks—*Where's the five bucks I gave you last week?*

- Gimme five bucks—Three hundred dollars a week for groceries is not enough.

- Gimme five bucks—I'm gonna win the lottery—I can feel it!

- Gimme five bucks—I need a Starbucks fix.

- Gimme five bucks—*No way! This is my last five bucks. You go to the ATM!*

Gimme. Gimme. Gimme. *I need. I need. I need.* If Abraham Lincoln ever knew he'd be in the middle of so many five-dollar civil wars, he would have gladly volunteered Robert E. Lee to place his mug on the five-dollar bill.

Before we got married, our marriage counselor told us that the four most common problem areas in marriage are communication, sex, family issues, and money. I could see that if a couple didn't communicate on important subjects like, "What's for dinner," then the husband would starve to death. And if a couple didn't have a healthy sex life, then the husband would starve to death. And if family didn't at least step up with decent wedding gifts for them, then the husband (and, in this case, possibly the wife) would starve to death.

But money? I wondered. *What could be the big deal about money?* If a couple can save some, give some, and spend some, what could possibly be the problem?

Of course, when we got married, we didn't have arguments about money because we didn't have any money. *Then I made my first five bucks.* Suddenly, the entire world economy teetered on financial collapse depending on what we did with that five bucks.

Now, everyone knows that it is a man's job to make money and a woman's job to spend it. After saying the two most dangerous words in the English language, "I do," a man goes from being a fiancé to a financier of his wife's spending sprees.

Any money he makes is hers. Period. When a woman runs out of cash, she will then place everything on credit only to hear her husband scream a month later, "What are all these unauthorized charges? Our last name is not Getty, Rockefeller, Forbes, or DuPont! AND THIS IS NOT THE WORLD BANK!"

For households where both spouses have income-producing jobs, the wife may have some leeway with her discretionary spending provided she makes more than $1.98 a week. In cases such as this, any money she makes is *hers*. The man cannot touch it unless he wants to risk an exploding ink cartridge going off in his hand. Any money the male money tree makes is still hers too. And if the wife makes more money than the man, what a coup! *Money, sex, and power are all in her grasp!*

It is a woman's marital and fiduciary right to purchase anything at any time. I don't know where it is in those prenuptial agreements, but it's in there somewhere. It doesn't matter if it is for her, the kids, or her friends, she's buying. Speaking of friends, what a racket that is. My wife and her friends all buy each other birthday, Christmas, Cinco de Mayo, and Groundhog Day presents. They are all bound by that weird female idea of social obligation I don't understand one bit. Talk about insider trading.

I don't buy my friends any presents and my friends don't buy me any presents. I can just see us talking behind each other's backs. "Did you hear what Phil bought Craig for Christmas? He got him the ugliest Hawaiian shirt. That man has the worst taste."

Women, you may have the cash and the credit, but we've got you cornered on your fancy financial footwork. If we would like to purchase something for ourselves, this is the gantlet we must run: (1) We must ask for permission. (2) Have the purchase amount approved. Any purchase over fifty dollars is subject to a credit report and the previous two years' tax returns. In this case, approval can take up to six weeks. (3) Check the remaining balance in the joint checking account to make sure it is higher than six dollars and thirty-seven cents. (4) Only make one transaction per month lest we be fined one hundred dollars, which will be credited to your personal checking account. If all these conditions are met, we can then go out and buy anything we please.

We all heard money maxims from our parents when we were growing up. These little truisms such as "A dollar earned is a dollar spent, uh, saved," "Money doesn't grow on trees," and "A fool and his money are soon parted" were repeated again and again to teach us the value of money. How come our parents never told us the money maxims for marriage?

"For richer" applies to the woman; "for poorer" applies to the man.

APR does not mean "All Prices Reduced."

Deposits must exceed withdrawals.

ATM fees, cash advances, and balance transfers add up.

Revolving credit spins out of control.

Sales are an evil corporate marketing ploy to entice your wife to spend more.

Now I admit that I've picked on women for a good part of this chapter so far, but I know guys like their toys. Guys tend to be harsh on their wives' spending sprees, but guys can also come up with the craziest, most extreme justifications for what they buy. If a guy can only make a couple of significant purchases in a year, he's gonna go big. Women break their spending into lots of smaller chunks, but guys make it count.

Guys go for the fishing boat. The motor home. The motorcycles. The Jet Skis. The complete Black & Decker workshop.

The big-screen TV for watching *Love Story*. The dual-head racing thruster cams with steel-alloy-turbo-charging commuter coffee cup holders. The oversize driver and irons. The home gym. Every wife has heard the famous last words, "Lookaddit this way, honey, we'll use this Hawaiian pig barbecue set all the time. *This'll last us forever.*" The big-ticket item will then be used once or twice in the next decade or until sold for one-sixteenth its value to make room for the next big-ticket item.

Common Ground

When you balk at your spouse's request for five bucks, chances are the ensuing argument isn't just about dollars and sense. Most married couples, when overcome with rational thinking and objectivity, know that arguing over five bucks doesn't make sense. It's a silly argument. We all know this. But try telling that to the spouse who says, "It's not about the money—it's the principle!" This line, we also all know, is a lie. It *is* about the money.

It's also about trust.

And security.

And freedom.

And control.

And individual responsibility.

And of course, five bucks are at stake.

You may have wished you married the millionaire next door, but the problem with money in marriage isn't moaning, complaining, or wishing you had more money. There are plenty of families with tons of money who have more financial problems than those who have very little money. I'm always amazed when I hear people who make six-figure incomes bemoaning the fact that they don't have enough money. Poor people.

The real problem lies with how you and your spouse handle what you have. Not only do you have to handle the money God has given you, you also have to handle how each other handles it. That's where the issues of trust, security, freedom, control, and individual responsibility come in.

Couples who don't share common ground with how money is earned, spent, saved, given, and invested are setting themselves up to go to extremes. Don't let your relationship go bankrupt by constantly arguing about money. Ask yourself and each other these important questions:

Do you and your spouse share the same philosophy regarding money in your home? Are you on common ground with your financial priorities? Do you consult with each other before buying big-ticket items? Do you have agreements about how money is spent on all the day-to-day items that add up to a big nut by the end of the month? Do you live within your means, or are you over your heads in debt trying to pay for a lifestyle you can't afford? Do you try to control each other instead of working together to control your money?

I once heard it said, "Money makes a good servant, but a poor master." Don't let money master, rule, and control your marriage. Get on common ground by identifying and communicating your financial priorities to one another. Invest in each other by honestly communicating your thoughts, feelings, values, and differences. Your marriage is too valuable to be wasted over financial frustrations. If finances are a weak spot for you and your spouse, learn how to get control of your finances by eliminating deficit spending. Cut up the credit cards if you have to. Discover the joy of giving by giving to your church and charity organizations. Come up with a spending plan and be accountable to one another. Learn to pay yourself first by developing a savings. Avoid spontaneous purchases. You can eliminate a lot of financial stress in your life by learning to live below your means.

Money has a funny way of showing how much you trust and believe in your spouse. Money also has a peculiar way of revealing how much you honor and respect each other's views about how to handle it. You can send the stock in your marriage soaring by mastering your money together. Arguing over five bucks or any other amount of money can drain the fun and joy out of your marriage, so make sure you are yielding positive dividends of trust and respect to your spouse on a regular basis. Getting on this type of common ground is what makes a marriage work.

Once you stop arguing over five bucks, you can send it to me.

I'm broke.

Let's Go Shopping!

21

Before marriage, a man yearns for the woman he loves.
After marriage, the "y" becomes silent.

Unlike a lot of guys, I must confess that I've read a lot of marriage books. The major buyers of marriage books are women, who then pass them on to their husbands and say, "Read this. We will be having a test in one week."

In our house, it's the reverse. I buy and read the marriage books and then pass them on to Krista. So far, she's ditched every test I've written. I am beginning to wonder if it's the book I selected, the combination multiple-choice/true-false questions on the test, or me?

No, a marriage book isn't like a Danielle Steele romance, a Dean Koontz thriller, or a John Grisham bestseller. Though not weighted with humor or blatantly honest like this book, most marriage books offer helpful and practical ideas for improving your marriage. I must take exception, though, with the one idea that seems to be a recurring theme in the numerous books

I've read. Somewhere, somehow, someone came up with the erroneous idea that *if* a guy really wants to make his wife happy and *if* he really wants to have a happy marriage, then he should go shopping with his wife. Excuse me?

Wives, do you *really* want your husband going shopping with you?

I mean, I can understand that when you need help hauling a new oak cabinet to your car, then a husband is a useful pack mule to have around. Or if you need your husband to pick out a new set of tires because if you don't pick out the correct steel-belted-waterproof-dual-aluminum-alloy mud-flingers, when you get home, your husband will send you right back to the tire store to get the correct ones put on.

But having your husband go shopping with you doesn't make sense for all sorts of reasons. First off, if your husband is a cheap tightwad who wouldn't lend his own mother a nickel, or should I say he's "frugal," then you're going to make each other miserable by inviting him to go shopping. If you do, you're asking for extremes. Guys like this who dream of second careers with the IRS are no fun to take shopping. Sure, you can tell the salespeople and strangers in line at the cash register that the guy following you around with a calculator is your trust fund accountant, but that ruse will only last so long. By the third or fourth store, your husband will eventually put a stop to your shopping spree by halting you at the register in a loud voice: "Enough already! You have to put *THIS, THIS, and THIS BACK!*"

Who wants to live like that?

If your husband isn't miserly, he may be one of those guys who suffer adverse physical symptoms whenever they spend too much time in a mall. Normally, a guy who physically reacts to shopping starts out with good intentions. Your husband wants to please you. He knows you want to spend time with him and he knows you like to shop. So, when you cheerfully suggest on a Saturday, "Let's go shopping," he agrees because he loves you. He knows this will make you happy, but inside he feels like he's teetering on a high wire over a thousand-foot chasm. Any number of things could go wrong on this shopping outing, all of which can send his body hurtling to the jagged rocks of sickness and infirmity down below.

You decide to go to the mall, and at first you're both in a chipper mood. Your husband is doing fine. The Muzak coming over the loudspeakers puts a little spring in his step. The soothing, gentle, bubbling sound of the water fountains eases any ripples in his spirit. The sound of laughing children brings a grin to his face. You feel confident that your husband will do just fine.

That is, until he walks into the first department store with SEMIANNUAL SALE, SALE, SALE signs plastered all over it. The place is packed. It's a madhouse filled with huge tables heaped with merchandise. Lost children are screaming for their mommies. Other husbands are walking around in zombie trances. There's one sales clerk for every two hundred people. Everyone is pushing and shoving. It is complete mayhem.

You look over at your husband. He seems pale. Droplets of sweat are forming on his forehead. He looks at you and gives you a faint smile with the reassuring words, "I'll be okay. You go on ahead. I'll wait outside the dressing room area."

You're not sure if you want to leave him alone, but when you look at all the deals around you waiting to be snapped up for oh so cheap, you can't help but figure he's a grown man who knows how to take care of himself. So you leave him to be swallowed by the merciless crowd.

Two hours later, you've landed bagfuls of fantastic buys and decide to rendezvous with your patient husband near the dressing room area. Along the way, you see a limp figure splayed out on a small couch looking as though he's just sat underneath a space shuttle launch. At first you think it's a mannequin ready to be thrown in the trash, but as you get closer, you realize it's your husband. He's nearly unconscious. His shirt is drenched with sweat. His eyes are glazed, lips cracked and parched. You wave your hands across his eyes, but you get nothing. You're not sure, but you think he may be on the verge of a Muzak-induced stroke.

As you sit him up in your arms, his eyes suddenly come alive as he whispers in a weak, croaking voice, *"Where ha-ha-ve youuuu beeeeeen?"*

You're not sure if you should call the paramedics, the coroner, or a mortician. Noting a couple of vital signs like breathing and a faint pulse, you opt for calling the paramedics. They quickly arrive and determine that your husband has suffered a Grand Mall seizure.

Not only is it a bad idea to take husbands shopping who are penny pinchers or prone to seizures, but the worst type of husband to take shopping is the one whose eyes are bigger than his pocketbook. Like a kid in a candy store, guys like this will run your family into the ground. That's precisely *why* you don't take them shopping.

In our town, we have one of those large discount shopping membership warehouses known as Costco, which is also called the Two-Hundred-Dollar Club. I don't care how hard you try, you can't leave the place without dishing out a couple of hundred bucks on stuff you marginally need (food excluded).

Take your husband shopping with you to the Two-Hundred-Dollar Club and it will quickly become the Apply for a Second Mortgage Club. A guy can go ballistic in these places. The first thing he sees is the big Jacuzzi hanging on the wall, and he thinks, *That's neat. We should get a Jacuzzi.* He's also thinking about what he read in the chapter, "It's Been a Long Time—" so he's ready for some creative romance. Never mind that the Jacuzzi costs a couple of grand, he pulls the purchase ticket and moves on.

You only came to buy bread, milk, fruit, and those tangy little sausage pizzas you just sampled from the little stand on the corner aisle, but your man is now on a mission. Summer is almost here! Before you know it, you have lost your husband. He was last seen with the largest forklift he could find, heading for the aisle with all the summer and garden accessories.

When you finally track him down, the forklift pallet is overflowing with a new patio table and chairs, a croquet set, an inflatable Olympic-size pool, a mesquite barbecue, water toys for the kids, a golf practice net, a teak umbrella, Kingsford coals, a side of beef, his and hers water skis, life jackets, and a twenty-two-foot Mastercraft ski boat.

"How are we going to pay for all this?" you ask in amazement.

"Relax," he says, "it's all a write-off."

Common Ground

Before you go broke, suffer a major seizure, or go to extremes over how much money you're spending, there are a lot of ways to spend time together without going shopping. In order for a marriage to stay on common ground, couples need to spend time together ALONE nurturing their love and admiration for each other. This is the important task of making your spouse your friend for life.

I believe that marriage is 5, maybe 10 percent romance, and the rest is all about compatibility. Nothing will enhance your feelings of compatibility and affection for your spouse more than a growing friendship.

Your marriage is more than just a partnership. It is more than just a love affair. It is more than just two people raising a family together. Your marriage is a lifelong commitment to nurturing and deepening a sincere, heartfelt friendship with your spouse. If you and your spouse work on being deeply committed friends to one another, you will see the other important areas like communication, romance, sex, and intimacy blossom in your marriage as well. It only makes perfect sense to get on common ground with your spouse as your best friend. Here are a few reminders on how to put friendship first in your marriage.

Be Affectionate. Nothing will stimulate feelings of affection and tenderness faster than physical touch. A warm hug. A strong back rub. Holding hands. A soft kiss. A playful pinch. Yes, even tickling. If you are affectionate with your spouse, you are sending him or her the clear message, "I like you." Liking your spouse is what compatibility is all about, and being affectionate stimulates those feelings of compatibility.

If you're a guy and you don't consider yourself to be very affectionate, understand that your wife needs to be touched. When you give her a gentle hug and tell her she looks pretty, you are making an investment in your friendship that will pay major dividends. Women need to be touched and held. They love it when their husbands hug them and make them feel secure. If you work on being affectionate with your wife, not only will you see her spark lit, you'll also find yourself drawn closer to her.

Spend Time Alone Together. Friends can drift apart because they don't spend time together, and the same is true for married couples. You both need time together away from work, away from the kids, away from major responsibilities, and away from the rest of the world to help your friendship grow.

This is where you and your spouse create your own unique memories. They are yours alone to be cherished and remembered. It could be a regular date night, a night away at a local hotel, or a full-blown vacation where the only thing you have to do is rest and relax together. For deepening your friendship with your spouse, there is no substitute for spending time alone together. And if you and your spouse like to go shopping alone together, well, all right, go shopping!

Be the Friend You'd Like to Have. People can get idealistic about what they want in a friend, but if you want to make your spouse feel secure and loved in your friendship, be the friend you'd like to have. If you'd like your spouse to speak in kind words to you, speak in kind words. If you value loyalty, be loyal to your spouse. If you want your spouse to respect you, respect your spouse. If you desire honesty, be honest. For everything you want in friendship, be that kind of friend to your spouse.

By being the friend you'd like to have, you are taking responsibility for your actions of friendship instead of expecting your spouse to act first. You will be putting into practice what the Bible calls "[honoring] one another above yourselves" (Romans 12:10). Friendship is all about honor, and if you honor your spouse above yourself, you'll have a friend for life.

It's My Way or the Highway

22

Marriage is a delightful form of combat where you get to sleep with the enemy.

It wasn't so long ago when, as kids, we stood in the checkout line at the grocery store and begged our moms for just one candy bar. In front of our tiny faces were dozens of colorfully wrapped packages of chocolate bars and chewing gum whispering seductively, "Buy me! Taste me! Eat me! If your mommy says 'no,' then get on the floor and throw a hysterical fit."

When we pleaded with our moms for just one teeny-eeny-weeny candy bar, but our mom said no, it'd spoil our dinner, what did we do? We did exactly what the candy told us to do— we went to extremes by flinging ourselves to the ground, writhing and screaming in a demonic tantrum to embarrass and bring shame to our cruel, candy-depriving mothers. What did our mothers do? They promptly scooped us up and gave us a big whack on the behind, for the sake of everyone else in the checkout line who had to endure our high-pitched wailing and foaming at the mouth. That was when spanking *was* politically correct.

Though a lot of couples don't like to admit it, every marriage has its own little games. Every married person has a way of getting what he or she wants in marriage. When a couple don't get what they want or need from each other, instead of just being honest and telling the truth, couples go to extremes by participating in immature, childish behavior. I know it's true. You know it's true. Your spouse knows it's true. There is a child in every one of us who is still begging for that one candy bar, and that little brat will do just about anything to get it.

Still don't believe me? Let's look at the following behaviors and see if they have any bearing on how husbands and wives try to get their own way.

Whining. Some spouses are whine connoisseurs. Take a sip of these whines and see if they've ever been stocked in your house—

I haaaate my hair.

Allll the guys are gonna beeeeeee there!

I feel soooooo ugly!

I've been cooped up in this house allllll daaaaay long.

I can't put up your shelves today. My baaaack is killing meeee!

It's yourrrrrrr turn to change the diaper!

If a spouse whines long enough about having ugly hair, an aching back, too much work to do, or not enough playtime, or about never getting to do what he or she wants to do, the other spouse will eventually begin to feel guilty, which is the exact purpose for whining. By whining, the conniving spouse presses the other's "should" button that sounds an inner alarm inside and provokes thoughts like—

Maybe I should lighten up. It's been a year since I've let him out of the house.

Maybe I shouldn't be so tight—I could see her face if she got a haircut.

Maybe I've misjudged him—if we buy a new TV, he won't always have it on.

Maybe I should let her get a new dress—the thrift store isn't what it used to be.

Whining is not gender- or chromosome-specific. Whining reinforces in the male or female mind that one spouse needs to be taken care of. There are plenty of men and women out there with the initiative and motivation and drive of Jell-O pudding.

So if a whining spouse's cards are played right, the other spouse will have the chance to be the more powerful and dominant spouse by coming to the other's rescue. Even though the whining spouse knows exactly what he or she is doing, part of this game is to appear forever grateful for the other's heroic rescue and amazing feats of inner strength. Thus, we see that whining is a cunning, manipulative tool used by one spouse to call the shots regardless of having to stoop to the level of pond scum.

Catastrophizing. When a spouse can't prevail through whining, he or she needs to resort to the greater extreme of creating a major catastrophe. This little trick works well when one spouse is at work, usually the husband. It goes something like this—

Ring! Ring! Ring!

"Hello, Ace Trucking. You crash 'em, we charge you big bucks to tow 'em away."

"Sam, this is Alice! We've got big problems, HUGE problems! Sammy spilled juice on the carpet!"

"And that's a big problem?"

"You don't understand—he spilled a five-gallon container of juice on the living room floor. Now we need new carpet. I've already figured it out. By the time we pay a carpet cleaner and get the carpet redyed, it would be cheaper for us to get new—"

"Wa-wa-wait a minute here, Alice. We are not buying new carpet. We already talked about that."

"*Sammy, NO!* Oh my goodness, Sam, Sammy just poured gasoline all over the living room furniture. It's ruined. Now we're going to need new furniture too."

"Alice, you know we can't afford new furniture."

"*Sammy! You put down those matches THIS INSTANT!* Sam, I gotta go. The living room is in flames. I have to rescue our son and get outta the house so we won't be burned to death and leave you alone for the rest of your pathetic life. Meet me at those new model homes with your checkbook."

Pouting. Whining and catastrophizing are overt, confrontational forms of marriage manipulation, but pouting is a more subtle, artful form of getting your way. Pouters crafted their skill as kids with weak parents who couldn't say no. Pouters are used to getting their way, and when they don't, their body language tranforms instantaneously—

Droopy eyes.

Long, sullen faces.

Hunched, burdened shoulders.

Apathetic stares into space.

Slow, labored steps.

Deep, heavy sighs.

Once a pouter's body language starts talking loud and clear, what follows are extreme, irrational statements like, "Nobody loves me, but that's okay. I'm used to it by now." "You go on ahead to our favorite restaurant without me. I'll be okay here with my chicken potpie." "Me? I'm fine. Nothing's wrong, really."

Ultimatumizing. If whining, catastrophizing, and pouting all fall flat, the last resort is the tried-and-true marriage ultimatum, "It's my way or the highway." Ultimatumizing is an all-or-nothing extreme designed to force compliance or conformity regardless of the consequences. This is when women take the high ground that they are always right and that it's time their husbands wake up and smell the café latte. This is when men claim they're never, ever wrong and they build their fortress walls with no-win questions their wives know better than to answer: "What do you think I am, stupid?"

A spouse who's prone to issuing an ultimatum over the smallest wish or desire is like that insipid little vermin named Veruca in *Willy Wonka and the Chocolate Factory,* who ground away at her father with ultimatum after ultimatum—anything to get her greedy little hands on an Everlasting Gobstopper. You remember her tantrums: "You're the meanest daddy in the whole world! *I want an Everlasting Gobstopper and if I don't get one, I'm going to die!*"

Everything goes back to the candy we never got.

Common Ground

What games do you and your spouse play when you go to extremes? What do you sometimes say and do that takes the place of honest communication? How could conflicts be minimized if you and your spouse spoke openly about your wants, needs, and desires?

You and your spouse may be really struggling in your marriage and resorting to all sorts of negative behavior to get each other's attention. That's no laughing matter. If you're in that position, your best bet is to meet with your pastor or a professional counselor to help you work out your marriage problems.

If you're like the rest of the married human race and you're willing to admit that you occasionally go to extremes by playing games with your spouse, here are three action steps you can take to pick yourself off the floor of the candy aisle and get on common ground with your spouse.

Deal with Issues Directly. No whining. No catastrophizing. No pouting. No my-way-or-the-highway. When you and your spouse are in conflict, deal with the specific issue at hand. Clearly state your perspective and position on the issue. Allow your spouse to do the same. Work together to develop resolutions that you both can live with. Be flexible and willing to negotiate. By dealing with issues directly, you avoid the game playing that may only lengthen the conflict and make it worse.

Husbands or wives that are wrestling with severe relationship, drug, alcohol, abuse, or morality problems typically use an ultimatum in a last-ditch effort to save the marriage, but an ultimatum generally serves no useful purpose for marriages that have not gone to those extremes. An ultimatum forces compliance, and compliance isn't a very good way to get on common ground.

Take Responsibility for Your Attitudes and Actions. When you've been hurt by your spouse, it's easy to want to lash back and get even. If they've said or done something mean or insensitive and if you allow yourself to stoop to their below-the-belt game-playing tactics, then they've won. Take the higher ground. Take responsibility for controlling your attitudes and actions when you and your spouse are in a fight. Refuse to react in a negative way. Show a greater respect for yourself and your spouse by insisting on accountability: "I refuse to be treated this way. We can resolve this problem whenever you cool down."

Sounds a bit righteous, I know. But outta line is outta line. By setting your boundaries about how you want to be treated when there's conflict, you will be letting your spouse know there is a better way and a higher standard for your marrriage. You'll also be making it very clear that you're not chopped liver. So there!

Be Willing to Forgive. Nothing will keep a marriage further away from common ground than bitterness, resentment, and unforgiveness. Withholding forgiveness from your spouse is the worst kind of game you can play in your marriage. It is a deadly poison that will drain the life and love out of both of you.

Everybody makes mistakes, and the only marriage without mistakes is a marriage made in heaven. Unfortunately, despite what some people believe, there's no such thing as a marriage made in heaven. There are only marriages made on earth, but through forgiving one another on a regular basis, that's bringing heaven right to your own home.

Though we love our spouses, we will say and do things that will hurt them. Though our spouses love us, they will say and do things that will hurt us. The best way to avoid the extreme of withholding forgiveness from your spouse is to take advice from God in heaven and "Forgive as the Lord forgave you."

Making up and moving on in your marriage only happens through authentic forgiveness. Though we don't deserve it, forgiveness is the one extreme God goes to every day on our behalf. Forgiveness will keep you from playing a game or issuing an ultimatum. Forgiveness is God's High Way and those who travel that road will never regret it.

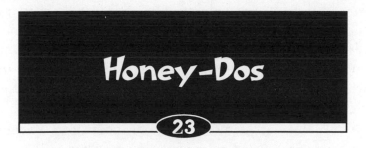

Honey-Dos

23

Marriage certificate is just another term for a work permit.

Like most guys, when I was growing up I had to do a lot of chores. My mom and dad were never prosecuted for violating child labor laws, but that's only because they had seven children. If there was anyone who understood forced labor, it was my mom. Don't get me wrong—I have great parents. At the time, I just didn't know they were preparing me for married life.

When my sisters and I were in elementary school, my father developed a program designed to teach us the value of a buck. Little did I know how I would come to appreciate, in my married years, the virtue of sweating like a dog in the broiling sun for a few George Washingtons. If I wanted a new tennis rackct, surfboard, or money to go on a ski trip, my dad would front me the money. All I had to do was work it off for a buck an hour.

Now, at nine years old, I was a lousy negotiator. I didn't know that if I wheeled and dealed for a buck and a quarter an hour, I could've shaved eight hours of manual labor off a forty-dollar tennis racket. Heck, all I cared about was my new skateboard or torture tools for my younger sister. So I agreed to a buck an hour and what my dad called his "indentured servant" program.

On Wednesday afternoons, I'd come home from Valentine Elementary School and go to work raking millions of leaves in the front and back yards, then mow the front and back lawn with our 1950s-era motorless grass clipper, paint the entire house inside and out, wash-n-wax-n-buff the red Country Squire station wagon with fake wood on the side, plant a few acres of corn, milk the herd, earthquake-retrofit the house in preparation for "The Big One," and reorganize the spice rack. After three hours of arduous labor, I earned—you got it— three whopping bucks.

Now that I'm married, a buck an hour doesn't sound like such a bad deal. Today's honey-do list is far longer than anything my parents could ever have dreamed up. And I get paid zilch.

In our home, Krista and I don't actually call these sexist chores the honey-do list. No, we're honest with each other— we call it what it is.

It's the "Do or Die List."

Hey, death is a good motivator. So is severe bodily injury. Pain motivates me.

Wives, if you want to understand why your husband moans and groans like a beached and dying manatee when you hand him the honey-do list just as he is throwing the golf clubs in the car, understand that you're basically dealing with a latent teenager. Most males, when slapped with a punch list longer than the yellow and white pages combined, are instantly trans-mogrified back to their youth with nightmarish visions of end-less weekend chores and stern parental warnings of "You're not going anywhere until your chores are finished!"

You hand him the honey-do list and his switch is flipped. You are no longer his wife, the bride of his youth, his beauti-ful betrothed. No, you are Helga the Labor Camp Enforcer. As a teenager, your husband was tortured by Helga with rakes, shovels, hoses, cattle prods, paintbrushes, window squeegees, pruning shears, and Ken dolls. Whenever he's handed a honey-do list, your husband experiences Post Traumatic Chore Dis-order. In this delusional state, your husband has terrifying flashbacks of being chased around his backyard by Helga the Labor Camp Enforcer, who's screaming like the Wicked Witch of the East, "IIIII'LLLL GET YOU, MY LITTLE PRETTY!!! YOU THINK THIS IS BAD? WAIT UNTIL YOU'RE MAR-RIED!! AAHHH-HA-HA-HA-HA-HA!"

Men like doing weekend chores about as much as cats like to swim. Guys hated chores as teenagers and guys still hate chores as husbands. Unless, of course, the chores are chores they want to do like dismantling the car, tying flies for a fish-ing trip, or dusting off the baseball card collection. In that case, a guy will call them chores, but you really know they're hobbies.

It's not that all men have bad attitudes when there's work to be done around the house. Any guy with reasonable intelli-gence knows darn well that when he's checking off items on the honey-do list, he's silently earning valuable brownie points redeemable for a ball game with the guys, the latest gadget he's been wanting for reasons you'll never understand, a WWF wrestling match, or sex. A man can become incredibly moti-vated to do chores when something he wants is at stake. If your hubby hasn't gotten around to fixing that hole in the screen door for the past six months, as his wife, you obviously haven't motivated him by pain or discovered what he wants. Why don't you get the kids out of the house, put on some perfume, slip into some lingerie, and knock 'im sideways with your most sultry voice, "Hey, Stud Muffin—how's about fixing that screen door? I'll be waiting when you're done."

Just watch Mr. Procrastinator instantly become Captain Screen-o-Matic.

Now we all know that husbands aren't the only ones who do work around the house. Women work until their fingers are bleeding and their knees are rubbed raw from hand-polishing the floor every day. Right guys?

But guys aren't the only ones who receive honey-do lists. Women get honey-do lists from their husbands, but they're of a different flavor. Guys don't make lists. Guys make deals.

Wives have honey-do lists. Husbands plead, "Aw, c'mon, honey."

The "Aw, c'mon, honey" phrase *always* precipitates a deal. And the "deal" is always situational. For example, you discover your toddler has downloaded soft-wear into his partially absorbent diaper. I say "partially" because anyone who has ever changed a BBB (baby bottom blowout) is acutely aware that whatever doesn't absorb, overflows. Instead of changing the baby yourself, you want to give your husband the opportunity to bond with his child. You take the diaper dilemma to your husband and say in your most diplomatic voice, "Here, it's about time you're trained in waste removal."

His reticent response goes something like this, "Aw, c'mon, honey—I'm tired—I'm terrible at changing diapers—I'll change Number 1, but not Number 2. You change this one for me and I'll promise to change the next Number 1."

Sound familiar?

Or what about taking the rented video back to Blockbuster? "Aw, c'mon, honey! You take it back. *Just this once.*"

Watching the kids for the evening, skipping out on visiting the in-laws in Chickasaw, unclogging the toilet, attending husband/wife socials under compulsion with people he doesn't know or care to know, filing tax returns, wanting to be waited on like British royalty while watching any sporting event on TV, paying the bills, or going to a girl movie with you are common task-avoidance opportunities for your husband to pull the "Aw, c'mon, honey" card. Especially when he has checked off every item on your honey-do list.

Common Ground

Every home in America is a sweatshop and deciding who does what around the house can produce major labor disputes. Before the honey turns sour in your marriage over division of labor responsibilities, why don't you and your spouse establish clear labor and support procedures for all the toil and moil that needs to be done around the house?

Remember: Common ground in your marriage changes over time. A work agreement that was perfectly good in the past may need to be revised. Maybe the two of you have clearly defined the roles and responsibilities regarding household chores, but these questions offer a new twist for things you may have not talked about in a while. Getting on common ground with household chores will help keep this important marriage issue from being swept under the rug.

- What chore(s) do you dislike, despise, or absolutely hate?

- What chore(s) do you prefer doing and don't mind doing at all?

- What is one chore you wish your spouse would do or at least share the responsibility for?

- How does your spouse react when you don't do what he or she asked you to do?

- How do you react when your spouse hasn't done what you've asked him or her to do?

- What type of support do you need from your spouse for chores?

- What are your kids learning from your attitudes and actions regarding chores?

Doing the dishes. Mowing the lawn. Getting the kids ready for bed. Doing mounds of laundry. Paying the bills. Driving the carpool. Fixing screen doors—hmm? Making meals. Putting away. Throwing away. Sweeping. Mopping. Dusting. Folding. Ironing. Clipping. Filing. Fixing. Enough already.

There's always more work to be done, and when the work finally gets done, you'll be doing it again in a few hours, days, or weeks. Pathetic, isn't it? That's why I believe one of the strongest measures of a good marriage is how the work gets done.

Your wife is not your mother or maid.

Your husband is not your personal valet or butler.

The work's gotta get done and you both gotta do it. The important thing is not to let chores divide your marriage by selfishness, laziness, broken promises, nagging, whining, or refusing to take responsibility for what you know needs to get done. Instead, you both need to identify what work has to be done around the house and what work has high priority, and then each be willing to negotiate, compromise, and pinch-hit when the other person needs help. With so much work to be done, how else can a marriage work?

Your husband or wife shouldn't have to earn your love as if working toward a degree in industrial engineering. Every wife, every husband gets fried from putting in long hours at the office or chasing and cleaning up after the kids all day long. For two-income families, multiply that by two or three. Depending on an individual's personality, likes and dislikes, strengths or weaknesses, some are bent to clean all day long like a fastidious Felix Unger. Others take the more casual Oscar Madison approach. Somewhere in between, there's a common ground and it's up to every couple to find it.

If you're looking for a good way to establish common ground, here's a good labor code for your home: "Let us not love with words or tongue but with actions and in truth" (1 John 3:18).

Don't let the chores around your house make your marriage a chore.

Honey-do can be a term of endearment if you're both willing to work at it.

That's Not Funny!

24

You want funny? I'll show ya funny!
—Moe

my wife hates *The Three Stooges.* I think Larry, Moe, and Curly are hilarious. Especially when this goofy trio are playing golf.

CURLY: Hey, ya moidered that ball, ya knucklehead! N'yuk, n'yuk, n'yuk!

MOE: Watchit . . . I'll show you who's a knucklehead . . . c'mere!

LARRY: Hey, guys, put down that club before someone gets hurt with it!

CURLY: Nnnnyyaa . . . betcha couldn't hit the side of a barn . . . n'yuk, n'yuk!

MOE: Oh yeah, lemme take a look at that club.

CURLY'S HEAD: *Doy-ooiiin-gga!*

Since a lot of women hate *The Three Stooges,* right now, I'm training my two daughters to like Larry, Moe, and Curly. Every week for the past few years, I have had a "Date Night" with my kids. We'll go to Mickey D's for Happy Meals or Wahoo's for fish tacos. Sometimes we'll rent a video or go down to the swings at the beach or go for ice cream at Dana Point Harbor. It's the one night of the week when the prisoners are in charge of the warden. It's also the same night my wife gets together with her girlfriends like she's been regularly doing for the past five years. Every Monday night, my wife gets in her car and our neighbors hear her rejoicing, "Free at last—free at last—thank God Almighty, I'm free at last!"

What she doesn't know is that every so often I'll pop in a *Three Stooges* video to teach my kids the fine art of eyeball poking and noogying as well as other embarrassing social behaviors. Shh, don't say a word to Krista—she'd kill me if she ever found out I was raising deviants instead of somewhat decent citizens.

For a long time, both sexes have known that guy humor is definitely not girl humor. Real guys are not that sophisticated. Smart women know this and that's why my wife refuses to watch even one minute of those classic Larry, Moe, and Curly reruns. Guys like physical comedy with a twist of violence thrown in. They like to see other guys shot up, thrown over bridges, and run over by trains. They like watching other guys taking their lumps. Getting smashed over the head with a golf club is funny, isn't it?

If you don't believe that guys are into stupid humor, ask any guy to recite one, just one line, from the old *Airplane* movies and in a split second you'll hear mimics and phrases like, "Sale at JCPenney," "Don't call me 'Shirley,'" or when the squeaky-voiced air-traffic controller pulled the plug on the runway lights—"Just kidding!"

Still don't believe me?

Mention two words and watch his face light up: *Monty Python*.

If that doesn't work, maybe your guy is a bit too serious and is lacking in the humor department. Give David Letterman a call and sign your husband up for "Stupid Pet Tricks." Guys have always been accused of being dogs and they'll do anything for food. Even dog biscuits.

Female humor is more intelligent than guy humor. Female humor deals with funny plots, character development, creative dialogue, perplexing conflict, and, most of all, *relationships*. That's what made Jane Fonda's *Nine to Five* such a blockbuster success for critical-thinking female moviegoers. She and Dolly Parton and Lily Tomlin sure won a whole lotta Academy Award votes for that one!

Though guys do like stupid, violent, or bodily function types of humor, there is a significant silent majority of women out there who do find humor in watching other women get what's coming to them. Don't believe me?

Ever see *Fatal Attraction?*

This female propensity to stick it to other women begins at a young age when little girls watch *The Wizard of Oz* for the first time. The moment the Wicked Witch of the West tries to steal the ruby slippers from Dorothy Gail of Kansas (that's a bit of trivia I betcha didn't know), all little girls intuitively learn that they, too, will one day meet their own Wicked Witch of the West. It is a terrifying realization, but they know it is a fate all women are powerless to prevent.

This villainous witch will appear in the guise of someone like Elvira Gulch who tried to take Toto away from Dorothy. It could be an eighth-grade science teacher, a sorority sister trying to steal her boyfriend, a female boss on a power trip, a PTA board member, or an old lady who's the president of her homeowners association. Even a fellow church member.

Upon meeting and clashing in an intense power struggle

with this vile, green-faced woman, the heroine (who we'll say is now your wife) will dub her new foe *"The Witch."* Your wife will make comments like, "This woman is evil. I know God says not to hate anyone, but I hate her with everything I have in me. I wonder what kind of broom she drives? She should be burned at the stake."

Being the funny kind of husband that you are, you're a bit taken aback by such extreme statements from your wife. So you take a little crack at humor to lighten your wife's invective vitriol.

"Do I hear you saying, dear, that she didn't like the cookies you made for the church bake sale?"

"Didn't like my cookies!?" your wife screams. "She hated my cookies! Right there standing in front of all the other moms, she said, 'These cookies taste like cat litter—who made these furballs?'"

Oops—you missed the funny bone—lions and tigers and bears, oh my!!

"I was so embarrassed I could die!" your wife cries. "What right did that *WITCH* have to critique my cookies in front of all my friends? And then, she started to pretend she was choking and everybody laughed. That woman is evil and we are never going to that church again!"

Of course, you think the woman's line about cat litter and furballs is hysterical, so you begin to laugh.

"That's not funny," your wife lashes and comes after you like one of those flying monkeys chasing Toto. You know you're not in Kansas anymore.

Common Ground

It's a good thing God has a sense of humor. After all, He gets to watch all the funny extremes we go to as husbands and wives. Guy humor is definitely different from girl humor, but laughter is the one thing you can't do without in your marriage. Couples who stop laughing, stop living. Laughter is a wonderful gift from God, and every couple needs plenty of it to make it through those crazy changes that happen in the course of marriage.

Laughter will make a radical difference in your life and in your marriage. Laughter puts life and problems into perspective when things go from bad to worse. Every marriage is destined to face struggles, job changes, moves, sickness, conflicts with in-laws, struggles with raising children, financial turmoil, grief, and heartache. All of these changes and conflicts in marriage are what cause couples to get knocked off common ground. Laughter will get you and your beloved back on the common ground of the things you mutually enjoy and cherish.

What in the world would you and your spouse do without laughter? Can you imagine walking into a park filled with kids and hearing only silence? What would people do on weeknights without their sitcoms? (Scary question!) How many families would be deprived of the Sunday morning funnies? Whoopi Goldberg, Goldie Hawn, Robin Williams, Billy Crystal, and Jerry Seinfeld would be out of work. *The Three Stooges* wouldn't be . . . don't even say it!

The thing I can't understand is, Why isn't the vow of laughter included in marriage vows?

When was the last time you and your spouse were dying of laughter? When was the last time you both shared a sidesplitting, tears-streaming, hyperventilating, on-the-verge-of-incontinence laugh? In this crazy, broken world we live in, laughter is a delicious reminder that you and your spouse are really alive.

I don't know about you, but when it comes to dying and dying of laughter, I'll take the latter. We all know the first one is bound to happen someday, but right now, some people are living like the walking dead and nobody can tell the difference. I may never appear on *Wheel of Fortune*, but I'll take a big "L" for $500, please.

Laughter is evidence of God's creative hand at work. Can't you imagine the thunderous laughter and excitement of God after He completed the creation of the world in a record-breaking seven days? I can just picture God leaning back in a lounge chair on a redwood deck overlooking all of creation on Sunday morning and hooting to Himself, "Boy, look at that . . . I did good . . . real good."

One of God's most wonderful creations was my best friend, Dana Robinson, who died eight years ago from lymphoma. Dana had one of the most joy-filled, contagious laughs I'd ever heard. He was such a joyful, friendly person that everyone wanted to be his friend and no one could ever get enough of him. Dana had the gift of laughter and shared it with everyone he knew.

Just the other night, I had a dream that Dana snuck up behind me and started laughing. I turned around, surprised to see my buddy, and cried, "Dana!" He kept laughing and laughing. It was so distinct. So pure. The most beautiful laughter I've ever heard. His laughter was so sharp and clear I could have sworn I was awake.

That dream was a wonderful gift from God, and laughter is a gift you can lavish on your spouse. It is the twin sister of joy and a sign of fire in the heart. It is the inexhaustible joy of God available to husbands and wives every day of their lives.

What do you and your spouse love to laugh about? What does your spouse find humorous that you don't, and vice versa? What is a creative way to incite a laugh in your spouse today?

If you and your spouse can't laugh about your marriage and the extremes you sometimes go to in order to get each other's attention, then you both need to visit a chiropractor to have your funny bones adjusted. Each day has seeds of laughter and it's your job to water 'em. Don't take each other so seriously. Laughter will help each of you keep your sanity and your marriage on common ground.

If you don't laugh, you and your spouse may wind up in the funny farm.

In Kansas.

With tornadoes.

And witches!

I Hate It When You Do THAT!

25

Why does a woman work ten years to change a man's habits and then complain that he's not the man she married?
—Barbra Streisand

My in-laws own a nudist mobile home park for retired people in Albuquerque, New Mexico.

Well, not exactly. Let me explain—

Krista and I and the kids recently went to Albuquerque to visit her side of the family. Her brother and sister-in-law. The aunts. The uncles. The Navajos. We were there to play golf, go hiking in the Sandia mountains, visit expensive shops we couldn't afford in Santa Fe, and torch our cerebral cortex on red chilies. Five days of doing the Southwest thang.

When we arrived at the mobile home park, we pulled alongside her brother's double-wide (that's mobile home insider's speak for two of those puppies smacked together). Michael and Joanne have a three-bedroom double-wide and that was to be the O'Connor tepee for the next four moons. Also traveling with us were my mother-in-law, Betty, and her husband, Milo. (Not of *Milo & Otis* fame.)

That evening, we all headed out the door to have Mexican food for dinner. The rental van was parked in front of two small storage sheds with a three-foot gap between them. On the other side of the fence behind the storage sheds was another mobile home, one of many in the park.

Well, as Betty, Krista, and the kids were piling into the van, I stood next to the van sliding door and observed the most bizarre sight. In two split seconds, a tall, elderly man with dark hair, about 6'3" or so, walked past the gap between the two storage sheds.

He paused for a brief moment and looked at me.

I caught his eye and stared back at him while my jaw dropped to the ground.

He was stark naked!

Like the old Sasquatch footage of Bigfoot pausing before disappearing into the brush, in an instant, the naked man disappeared.

I stood there shaking my head, checking my eyesight, making sure that what I really saw was really what I saw.

I dashed over to Milo and Joanne, who were getting in her truck, and cried, "Joanne! I just saw a naked man on the other side of that fence! Right there! In front of us—just a second ago! What's that guy thinking?"

I was indignant. I wasn't going to spend the next four days parked next to some old guy baring his double-wide every day. Not my idea of family entertainment.

Joanne apologized and said, "Yeah, that guy's a little weird. Michael says he's been doing that, but we've lived here for a whole year and I've never seen him do it."

That's it, I thought. Arrest the guy! Brand him where it counts!

Being an in-law didn't give me much authority at the

mobile home park, so over dinner, I expressed my incredulity to Betty about the visual violation that had traumatized me.

Betty said, "Yeah! I'm going to tell Michael to put a notice in that man's file! He can't be running around the park naked like that!"

Unfortunately, Michael wasn't around to hear me rant on about eviction notices and child protection laws and epidermis so white I needed to put on my sunglasses. He was away at a tennis tournament and wouldn't be returning until the next day.

When Michael returned, I sure gave him the naked truth.

"Michael, that guy can't be walking around his yard naked! That's not right! Do you know what this New Mexico sun will do to his skin?"

Betty piped in and said, "Michael, I want you to put a notice in his file. If he does it again, I'm going to evict him."

Michael laughed and responded, "No way—that guy livens this place up. He's the only one in this park who's doing anything exciting."

The rest of us laughed as we realized how slow life must be in a mobile home park for retired folks.

I got off my high horse and quipped, "Okay, I guess we could turn the other cheek."

Common Ground

If that naked Bigfoot was married, I bet walking around the garden like that drove his wife absolutely berserk. I can just imagine his wife peering out the side door and whispering in a raspy voice, "George! George! You get back in here! I told you if you walk around our backyard naked one more time that I'm gonna lock this door. You know I *hate* it when you do that!

I'm sick of the girls in my bridge club making fun of my husband. Now you get right back in here and put some clothes on. George, I know you can hear me—get back in here this instant! Okay, fine, have it your way, Mr. Nudie No Shoes. See if you'll get any suntan lotion from me. No way, uh-uh, you're gonna fry that bum of yours!"

Guys, this isn't something I recommend you try in your backyard.

This man was a trained professional.

I don't know what personal idiosyncrasies, gross habits, or peculiar behaviors drive your spouse crazy, but what husband and wife haven't yelled at each other, "I hate it when you do that!"

Hopefully your spouse doesn't yell that at you the moment you wake up every day, but let's be honest for a minute. Every husband or wife has a few pet mannerisms or behaviors that drive the other person bonkers. These behaviors aren't what you read about in typical marriage books. Those other marriage books never even mention revolting habits, or if a slight reference to them is made, the writer asks you to blindly "accept your spouse's personal differences." That's a safe, hermetically sealed, antiseptic way of hiding the naked truth. Not in this book! No way, here is where I air all the dirty laundry about the private lives of American marriages.

Wives, does your husband know how to use toenail clippers, or does he pick at his smelly toes while you're trying to read in bed? (My wife can empathize with women who escape into romance novels.)

Guys, does your wife refuse to burp in public restaurants all in the guise of being a decent, well-mannered human being, but as soon as you get home, she unleashes the smell of the pastrami sandwich she had for lunch like a roaring foghorn?

BAAARRROOOOOGGGAAAA!!!

Who gets the downstairs couch when the other person is snoring loud enough to drown out a Santa Fe locomotive?

Who's the neat freak in your home? Which one of you stays up until one A.M. scouring underneath the toilet before waking up at six A.M. to leave for a week's vacation? Granted, being a fastidious cleaner isn't a gross habit, but it does tip the obsessive-compulsive scales. We have all heard that psychiatrists refer to this behavior as "anal retentiveness." That word combo alone is enough to make me feel sick to my stomach.

What about zits? Who's the zit picker in your home? Who is the family dermatologist, you or your spouse? How many intimate moments in bed have been completely ruined by one spouse looking at the other's back and exclaiming in awe, "Wow! Look at the size of that thing! Lemme at it—it's going to blow higher than Krakatoa, East of Java!" We don't even have enough space in this book to bring up the subject of ingrown hairs.

Which one of you chews your fingernails until they are raw, bleeding appendages—or mines for earwax as though it were a commodity traded on the Chicago Futures Exchange—or jams a finger so far up your nose that the fire department has to rush over to remove it with the "jaws of life"?

Sick, you say, *completely disgusting.*

That's right, marriage is filled with gross and disgusting habits. I'll spare you all the wild ideas I came up with regarding other bodily functions because I know some readers can only handle this material in baby steps. In fact, marriage has so much aberrant behavior that I think every dating and personal introduction service should have a required section on their application forms with the heading: GROSS AND DISGUSTING HABITS. Every single person would then know *exactly* what they're getting themselves into.

And to think we are made in the image of God—Lord, help us.

When you take an honest look at all these nauseating habits, they make public nudity look like a walk in a mobile home park. (I couldn't bring myself to survey couples to nail down the Terrible Top Ten Habits—I was terrified to discover what I'd find.)

So what are you to do when your spouse has a habit that drives you crazy and refuses to stop? You know for certain that's one piece of real estate you have no desire to be on common ground with. Here's a bright idea: Turn the other cheek.

I'm really serious here. You may have to leave the room in order to avoid being sicked out, but turning the other cheek to your spouse's idiosyncrasies begins with recognizing that you may have habits that disgust your spouse as well. By making a big deal out of your spouse's habits, according to current dysfunctional thinkers, you only empower that behavior. Don't stoop below the stuff between your toes. Work at fixing your own habits instead of picking on or at your spouse. Refuse to make the other's extreme your extreme.

Now, if you are an offending spouse (I do include myself in this category) and your husband or wife has no blatantly bad habits, take it from an extreme idiosyncratic inhuman beast like me: Get over it! If you really want to show you care about your spouse's thoughts and feelings, keep your peculiarities to yourself. If you have a certain habit your spouse hates, why push it to extremes? Bad habits are the quickest way to push your spouse's extreme button. Like bad breath, they make you unapproachable, unrefined, and undeniably unattractive. Is your spouse really to live under this oppression for the next forty years?

"I hate it when you do THAT," is a clear warning whistle for behavior begging to be changed. Instead of bugging your spouse to extremes, find something they like and make a new habit of doing it on a regular basis.

Do a chore without having to be asked.

Tuck secret notes inside their purse or briefcase.

Let 'em sleep in on the weekend.

Buy a simple but special gift.

Make their favorite meal.

Tell them the things you like most about them.

Plan a surprise weekend away.

Get rid of that habit that really bugs 'em.

Develop these habits or breathe some positive, life-giving habits of your own into your marriage. Soon you'll hear your spouse say with thanksgiving, "I *LOVE it when you do that!*"

You Rile the Kids Up, You Put 'Em to Bed!

26

Be nice to your kids. They'll choose your nursing home.

Who says guys don't know how to put the kids to bed? It's high time someone put this dastardly dad discrimination to rest. For years, guys have had to prove that they are both competent and capable at getting their kids to bed. I mean, how hard is it to get kids dressed, brushed, pottied, prayed, and tucked into bed?

Yes, every guy knows that his wife can zip through this necessary nightly ritual in less than ten minutes, but what's the big hurry? Guys know that their wives want to get the kids to bed early not because the kids need their rest, but because Mom needs hers—and besides, she wants to watch her favorite sitcom. Why make putting the kids to bed such a hurry-up-and-get-to-sleep system? Why make it so predictable? So routine? So one-dimensional? So boring.

Kids need to expand their horizons. They need their minds and bodies to be shaken and invigorated from that Jell-Oinduced state caused by too much TV and Sega. They need to push the limits. Break the envelope. Maybe even break (moms will love this) the sound barrier. Kids need to go to extremes, and that's why God made dads.

Let's take a vote: Ask your kids who they'd prefer putting them to bed, Mom or Dad? Hands down, Dad wins. Kids love it when Dad puts them to bed because that means they'll get to stay up *at least* forty-five minutes longer.

Start with "peeyamas." Once he gets his kids into their bedrooms, the first major challenge the dad faces is *finding* his kids' peeyamas. For all he knows, the peeyamas could be in a drawer, a closet, a Barney suitcase, a wastebasket, or a hamper, or (most likely) under the bed. How is he supposed to know where his kids put their peeyamas? Once the peeyamas are located, the dad enters his first major battle of the evening when he squares off with his three-year-old daughter who insists on choosing which pair of peeyamas she wants to wear.

"Honey, wear the Tinkerbell jammies."

"No, I wanna wear Winnie Pooh."

"Aw c'mon, just wear the Tinkerbell jammies. They look so cute on you."

"I hate Tinkerbell!"

"We don't say that word in this house. Winnie Pooh never says that word."

"Okay, but do I have to wear the Tinkerbells?"

Sad, pleading, puppy eyes.

"I guess not—you can wear the Winnie Poohs."

Even though her head doesn't fit through the opening for the right arm, the little DWARF (Daddy Wrapped Around Right Finger) insists she can put on the Winnie Pooh jammies just fine on her own. Winnie Pooh ends up backward and inside out, but she declares, "I meant to do that."

Knowing better than to mess with a willful woman, the dad sits back on his haunches and waits. Having already lost two battles, the dad now needs to compensate by launching a Tickle Monster counteroffensive. Seeing his daughter in her jammies makes it completely impossible not to tickle her. The dad was created for this purpose.

As she squeals in high-pitched laughter, his older son tears into the bedroom, wearing Photon Destroyer peeyamas and screaming, "DEATH TO THE ALIEN SLIME SUCKERS," whereby he proceeds to knee-drop dear old Dad to the floor. The dad plays dead and allows his kids to pound on him for 7.8 seconds. Like a phoenix rising from the ashes, the dad yells in a thundering voice, "BLANKET RAID!" His kids scream loud enough to break the neighbors' windows and his wife, who happens to be watching her favorite sitcom downstairs, shakes her head and tells herself not to get up.

Quick as a flash, Dad grabs the covers off his daughter's bed and, in one fell swoop, covers both kids who are now kicking and screaming like cats in a bag. Inevitably, both kids konk heads and Winnie Pooh begins crying.

"Okay," the Instigator asserts with a voice of authority and control, "settle down now."

Time to brush teeth.

Younger kids hate, oops, dislike using minty toothpaste because most dentist-recommended toothpaste feels hotter than Arizona asphalt in the middle of August. "It's too spicy," the kids cry as bubbly green foam drools down their faces.

Dads have a quick remedy for toothpaste burn victims. *Entertain them.* Putting a healthy dab on a toothbrush, the dad will work up a big glob of gooey foam and proceed to make toothpaste foam bubbles larger than his face. Not all dads aspire to such heights. Other variations on a theme include: Crazy Man Foaming at the Mouth, Foam on the Mirror, Foam Spit Tricks, and Foam Grenade.

Potty time.

During the potty portion of the bedtime routine, if Mom's in charge, the kids always have to go Number 1. If Dad's in charge, the kids always have to go Number 2.

Always.

From a physiological point of view, this is because twenty minutes of jumping on the bed, wrestling, and tickling produce enough activity to get the lower intestine moving and grooving.

From a psychological point of view, kids know that by sitting on the potty they can eke more time out of going to bed. By claiming to have to go Number 2, even giving the slightest mention of Number 2, they buy time because there's no way the dad is going to take any chances.

"You just sit there, honey, and take all the time you need. Wanna book?"

Now for prayer time.

Prayer time is a major spiritual event in our home. One time when I was saying prayers with Ellie, our four-year-old, I felt a distinct little swipe across my forehead. I opened my eyes and looked at Ellie, who had a sneaky smile on her face.

"Ellie, what did you just do? Why'd you touch my forehead?"

"I wiped my goop."

That nostril deposit incited a furious tickling match and delayed prayer time another few minutes, which led to another series of distractions.

Distractions are what make it difficult for dads during prayer time. They're not used to fielding so many difficult questions. What is a dad really supposed to say when his kids ask how God turns the rain on or what Jonah looked like after he spent three days in the belly of a whale or why Noah allowed cockroaches and mosquitoes on the ark? Dads have a tough time answering such theological questions.

"Well, son, cockroaches play a very important role in making God laugh. You know how your mother and sisters jump up on the chairs and start screaming whenever they see an itty-bitty cockroach. God thinks that's funny and that's why He created cockroaches. They're also the only ones who'll eat your mother's cooking, but that's just between us men."

By the time the fifth glass of water has been drunk and 473 monsters have been killed under the bed, in the closet, and outside the window, and the eleventh "Just one more question—" has been answered, it is an hour and forty-five minutes later, but the kids are exhausted and go right to sleep. The sitcom is long over and the dad's wife is fast asleep.

See, that wasn't so bad.

Piece of cake.

Common Ground

Putting the kids to bed isn't the only area in which wives get worried about their husband's caretaking skills. It would take a long time to tell what *really* happens when Mom goes away for the weekend. So far, wives only have general ideas of what goes on when they're gone. They think that the kids wear the same clothes all weekend (true) and that the only meals the kids eat are cereal and Happy Meals (true) and that their husbands stock up on Blockbuster videos (true) and that several near-accidents involving hot waffle irons and fingers, broken glass, snail poison, and climbing on the roof are narrowly averted (all true), but if wives ever really found out what happens with Dad and the kids when they're away, WOOHOO, boy, would that unpack their bags!

Kids play a major influence in the lives of husbands and wives. Though kids don't realize it, it's absolutely crucial for married couples never to underestimate how much time, attention, and energy are devoted to raising children. As wonderful and awesome a privilege as it is to nurture the growth and development of children, couples need to realize that *too much* attention focused on the children *at the expense of the marriage* will eventually squeeze the life out of the marriage. Sounds crazy, but it's true.

Your kids are important, but the best gift you can give them is modeling a healthy marriage. Kids today need to see their parents with a deep love and respect for one another. They need to see Mom and Dad spending time alone in quiet conversation. They need to see Mom and Dad going out alone together on dates. They need to see Mom and Dad take short trips away together. They need to see that it's okay for Mom and Dad to have their differences and be able to work through conflict in healthy ways. They need to see a dad who gives Mom emotional support and practical help around the house. They need to see a mom who respects and supports her husband in his work. They need to see Mom and Dad give their best energy to one another first. (Or at least a few days a week!)

I'm afraid too many couples have it completely backward today. How many couples do you know who spend all their time running their children from one after-school activity to the next? When the weekend comes around, it's all-day soccer, baseball, gymnastics, church, and just about any other imaginable event that leaves the family as frazzled as during the week. With a crazy, hectic schedule like that, some husbands and wives don't have any physical or emotional energy to invest in each other. They are so obsessed with their kids' performances in school, sports, church, clubs, and other activities that the marriage takes a backseat to raising high-octane, high-performing kids.

Why is this? There could be loads of different reasons, but here is one I find most compelling—*many parents lean on their kids for the emotional boost that's lacking in their marriage.* If a marriage has gotten off common ground and is foundering somewhere in the doldrums of neglect or indifference, it's a whole lot easier to expect and receive emotional strokes from a child who pleases you than from a spouse who isn't meeting your specific needs.

Do all couples with busy kids have less than healthy marriages? Of course not. But *it is easy for couples to slip into unhealthy patterns of overcommitment without realizing it.* Positive and enriching activities are certainly a necessary part of a child's development. The real question is, How many and how often?

If you want a healthy marriage, you and your spouse must set personal and family boundaries for what your kids do and when. Know when to say "No" and know when to say "Yes." Make sure that your highest priorities for your marriage are in order by talking about the balance between healthy, nurturing activities and overcommitment. Look over your calendar and purposely plan to have slow seasons during the year with your kids. Don't forget to mark off in red ink special times away together. Don't let your kids' activities determine the pace of your marriage. Let your marriage set the climate for purposeful activity for your whole family. Give your best energy to your spouse, and you'll discover that there will be plenty left over for the kids. Even if they get to bed late.

You Work Too Much!

27

Trying to clean up after kids is like
shoveling snow in a snowstorm.
—Phyllis Diller

Work.

It's one of the most common points of contention in married life. On a daily basis, couples all across America get up, go to work, and get worked up at each other over work. Housework. Kid work. Work work. Work is an equal opportunity employer. You'd think that for something so many people hate to do, they'd spend less time arguing over it.

Now, I don't think most couples like to argue over work. Who wants to go to extremes over an unavoidable, necessary part of life? Married couples have always argued about work, but work has changed a lot over the past few decades. In traditional homes during the 1950s and 1960s, many arguments about work began with a simple, innocent question asked around the kitchen table. Many of the most extreme arguments regarding work started as innocuously as this—

HUSBAND: Honey, I'm home!

WIFE: Hi, dear, how was work today?

Husband slams briefcase down on kitchen table.

HUSBAND: Work stinks! I'll never amount to anything in this loser job!

Wife looks at big scratch on kitchen table she just refinished with three coats of lacquer and thrusts hands to her hips.

WIFE: Look what you just did! Do you know how long I worked on that table?

HUSBAND: Not as long as I've been slaving away at the office.

WIFE: That's a terrible thing to say. Well, if you think your work is over for the day, buddy-boy, have I got a list for you! After you sand and repaint that scratch—

HUSBAND: Save it for the weekend. I've got to be back at the office in an hour. Somebody dropped the ball on the project—

WIFE: Oh no, you don't! You're not going anywhere until that scratch is fixed!

HUSBAND: Look, I'm sorry I scratched your table, but you know how terrible I am at fixing scratches. All I've got time for is a quick bite.

WIFE: My table?! What ever happened to *our* table? This is the table we bought together when we were first married— *we never sit together at this table anymore. I love this table and—*

Cut! We'd better stop June and Ward from arguing before the Beav walks in.

Nowadays, with two-income families, work-related arguments escalate into extremes like this—

WIFE: Honey, I'm home.

HUSBAND: Hi, honey, I'm home too.

HUSBAND & WIFE: Did you pick up the kids?

Both spouses slam their briefcases down on the kitchen table and simultaneously scratch the table.

HUSBAND & WIFE: Look what you just did!

WIFE: Don't try to change the subject—we had an agreement!

HUSBAND: You said you'd pick up on Monday, Wednesday, and Friday if I dropped off and picked up on Tuesday and Thursday.

WIFE: Today is Thursday!

HUSBAND: No it's not—today's Friday!

WIFE: Is not!

HUSBAND: Is too!

Husband and wife check kitchen calendar together and scream—

OHHH NOOOO—IT'S SATURDAY!!!

If one or both spouses have been accused of working too much in the modern American home today, another extreme that occurs is when one spouse feels jilted for not getting enough recognition or appreciation for the contribution they make in the family. Typically, this is the wife who is a stay-at-home mom who sometimes feels guilty for staying at home (as opposed to the perpetually-stays-in-guilt mom-who-feels-guilt-from-her-kids-who-do-a-darn-good-job-making-her-feel-guilty-for-not-staying-at-home-feeling-guilty-for-not-having-a-"real-job").

The unappreciated wife is often made to feel this way by an overachieving, workaholic husband when he waltzes in after spending a long and arduous day in team meetings on the golf course.

HUSBAND: I'm home—guess what, dear? That next-generation computer chip I designed to rid the planet of pollution won another major industry award and the owner of the company just gave me forty million dollars in stock options. Better yet, I even shot a perfect round of golf with three hole-in—*WOULD YOU TAKE A LOOK AT THIS HOUSE! WHAT HAVE YOU BEEN DOING ALL DAY?*

WIFE: Look at me like that again and I'll rip a hole in your head the size of Pebble Beach—what do you mean, "What have I been doing all day?" You wanna know what I've been doing, *I'LL TELL YA WHAT I'VE BEEN DOING.* Picking up the clothes you dumped on the floor yesterday. Taking your smelly shirts and suits to the dry cleaners. Buying the gopher traps for the rodents that are destroying my garden, the ones you promised to kill last week. Taking two sick kids to the doctor, one of whom vomited in the car on the airline tickets for our trip to the Caribbean I'm not sure I want to take with you! Then, by the time noon rolled around—

HUSBAND: Okay, okay, so you had a rough day—you won't have to worry about that anymore now that we can afford a maid. Now you can go back to work like we've talked about—

WIFE: Back to work? What do you think I've been doing the past few years? Practicing putting in my office like you?

HUSBAND: Wuh-wuh-well, it's not like you need a degree to be a mom—

KA-POOOWW!

Common Ground

Workaholic husbands and unappreciated wives. Those are only two divisions of labor issues made in America. What about women in the professional-for-pay workforce who do double duty with home and office responsibilities? Or military and sales positions that require a lot of travel and leave the other spouse feeling like a single parent? Or an oppressive job environment where one spouse lives under the tyranny of an ogre boss? Or when a company requires a family to move across the nation in order to keep a job? Or what about unethical business practices? The punch list goes on and on—

Work is a major part of every marriage and if you want to make your marriage work, you have to be willing to work on how you work. Unless you are a lottery winner or trust fund baby, you and your spouse will spend the majority of your lives working.

Understanding how to keep work from pushing your marriage off common ground will help you keep your most important priorities in line.

Guys put a lot of stock in what they do. In large part, their sense of personal identity and their self-esteem are rooted in what they do. They measure their success, accomplishments, and sphere of influence by sales quotas, growth of the company, or growth of their ministry—by what they do. When introduced to a stranger, this is the first question a guy is usually asked, "What do you do?" Most men want to give a decent response to this question. "Duh—" is not an appropriate response.

Guys also have a definite fear of not being able to provide for their families. If a guy works for a company, there's always the fear of being mowed down by the company. If a guy owns his own company, there's always the fear of being mowed down by the competition or, worse, sued by one of his employees who fell out of his chair and injured himself while sleeping on the job.

Take away a guy's job or have a business go down the tubes and you've got one hurtin' puppy. The guy's embarrassed. Searching for options. Afraid of putting his family in the poorhouse. Scared of failure. Afraid of unknown changes. Wondering about the loss of approval and acceptance of others. And now scrambling to get another job before someone asks him that dang question about what he does for a living.

Guys have a deep need to be respected for what they do. The respect of others, and especially their wives, is intricately linked to how they feel about their jobs. This happens all the time when I'm working on a new book. I'll say, "Krista, listen to this—" and read something I wrote that I think, or at least hope, is funny. What I want her to say is, "Oh my goodness, that was incredibly brilliant. Why hasn't Letterman or Leno called you yet?" What I want is her approval and for her to sign off on my work by saying, "Go with it, it works."

When she sends me back that blank stare that silently says, "I can't believe I actually married this man," that key nonverbal cue tells me: (1) What I just wrote was not only *not* funny, but stupid. Not only was it stupid, it was *stupid* stupid. (2) I'd better get back to the drawing board and work harder. (3) Or get a real job.

What wives want most from their husbands is appreciation. Many women work because of the financial need to cover the living expenses that can't possibly be covered with one income. In this case, women often feel torn between work and home, and it doesn't help to have an unappreciative husband. It's expensive to live in today's world, but the one thing a woman values, whether she's able to stay home, has to work, or chooses to work, is appreciation from her husband who recognizes what she does as important.

If you want your wife to respect you for your work, you can demonstrate your respect for her work by heaping on her a hearthful of appreciation. Raising kids is a 24/7 job that never ends, and so if you are generous with praise, you'll see it boomerang back to you tenfold. Look at what your wife has done instead of what hasn't been done. Instead of criticizing, offer your help and support. Some days, moms have complete blowouts that would frazzle the toughest salesman, the meanest truckdriver, or the most heartless defense attorney. Juggling kids, carpools, practices after school, errands, chores, meals, and meetings is a lot of work. *Important work.* Praising and appreciating your wife is one pursuit you can never take to extremes. Your kind words will remind her how special and important she is to you.

Making your husband or wife feel appreciated for who they are and what they do is a key ingredient for a happy marriage. Marriage takes work and a great marriage takes a lot of work. By respecting and appreciating what your spouse does, you will fortify the common ground that you share together. Strengthening the common ground in your marriage will take a lot of sweat and tears, but it is definitely worth the work. Even if the kitchen table scratch never gets fixed.

You Always Take Your Family's Side

28

does your husband have any recent dental records?"

"Dental records," Krista asked. "Why would you need dental records at a time like this?"

Imagine you're about to have your first baby. You're eight months pregnant and you're sitting in the living room of your small, two-bedroom condominium wondering where in the world your husband could be. Sitting across from you is a Sergeant Joe Friday "Just the facts, ma'am"–type police investigator asking dozens of innocuous questions about the disappearance of your husband, who went rock climbing yesterday up a steep thousand-foot granite mountain.

The day before, I had left for the small mountain community of Idyllwild near Palm Springs with two climbing buddies to go rock climbing for the day. Our objective (a term to be used lightly when discussing rock climbing, bomb defusement,

217

and naked men in mobile home parks) was to climb a majestic thousand-foot rock named Tahquitz, which stood like an imposing tower over Idyllwild. Only three weeks earlier, I had climbed it for the first time with another friend and we completed that climb in three hours. This time, though, we had two ropes and three climbers, which slowed us down like a late afternoon L.A. traffic jam.

"Don't stop! Keep climbing—it's almost dark."

Todd's voice echoed up the granite rock face as I stood on a small ledge pulling up my rope a hundred feet above him and Rich. The orange summer sun had set over an hour before. I was in the lead and desperately scanning the shadowy rock for the next crack system to climb. Slung over my shoulder, carabiners, wire stoppers, camming devices, and belay rings gently clinked like a metal wind chime.

My watch glowed 8:45 P.M. as I placed the next piece of gear into a vertical crack. *That'd better hold,* I thought as I pulled myself up the next section of rock. Still 150 feet from the top, I wished we had several of those Hollywood premiere searchlights illuminating our way. (Rock climbing in the dark isn't a good idea if you ever want to see the light of day again.)

The charcoaled shadows that blanketed the massive peak sent a nervous rush of adrenaline through my system as I realized there was no way we were getting off this mountain tonight. When I belayed Todd and Rich up, the three of us tied into the same small tree on the side of the cliff you've seen in dozens of cartoons. Yes, it does exist. The three of us bivouacked there for one long, freezing night with no food, no water, no jackets, and no cell phones for a quick call home. Todd and I commented often how much our wives were going to kill us when we got home. By 11:00 P.M., I figured Krista was probably already shopping for a new Smith & Wesson. And a box of armor-piercing bullets.

Early the next morning, Krista called the police and filed a Missing-Husbands-Soon-to-Be-Flogged report. An hour or so later, the investigator arrived at the door and began asking perplexing questions about dental charts.

"Well ma'am, in rock climbing accidents, teeth are about the only thing left over to identify the body. That's why we need dental charts."

That's exactly the kind of comforting reassurance my pregnant wife wanted to hear. Did that detective have the gift of sensitivity or what?

After spending a frigid night like three huddled apes in a tree, at daybreak we climbed the remaining hundred feet, made it off the mountain and hiked down to our car. Strangely absent were the search and rescue parties.

As we drove to the ranger station in town (just in case they had to call off the assembled reconnaissance teams from all four branches of the armed forces), we developed our own pet theories as to why no one out of three families came to get us sooner. Ideas ranged from—

"Like Tom and Huck, they're waiting for us to show up at the funeral."

"They didn't notice we never came home."

"They *did* notice we never came home and they're throwing a party."

"They took a vote and with one voice declared, *'LET THEM ROT!'*"

Our welcoming party was a lynch mob. The news of our safety was greeted with sighs of relief from our wives, families, and friends. And the sound of clicking revolvers. My father, who is a funeral director with strong feelings about death and the sanctity of life, was ready to make scrap metal out of my climbing gear. I kept telling him that a noose isn't the safest type of climbing knot.

Common Ground

For years, rock climbing was an extreme sport I loved and never could get enough of. When I developed tendonitis in my wrists from that other extreme sport known as typing, my rock-climbing days were over as quick as an icy avalanche. Not wanting to be a widow, Krista thanked the Lord for my wrist problems, which I thought were a bit more extreme than rock climbing.

Though I don't rock climb anymore, I still have a passion for the outdoors and the practical lessons it teaches us about life. Rock climbing is about problem solving and marriage is a lifelong process of learning how to solve problems together. The important question for couples to consider is what kind of or *whose* problems they want to solve.

When Todd, Rich, and I sat overnight on that big rock, we caused a lot of trouble for our families, and family troubles are one of the most common areas in which couples go to extremes. In this case, I'm talking about extended family problems, which are those problems outside your spouse and children. Dealing with parents, grandparents, ex-spouses, in-laws, brothers, sisters, aunts, uncles—all the way up or down the family tree—can drive husbands and wives bananas. Flat ground isn't always common ground and for families in conflict, there's more than a few of you who'd rather be roped way up high to a tiny little tree.

Scaling extended family problems is often like scaling a thousand-foot rock face. You can only tackle what's in front of you. You have a limited number of options. The only equipment you have is what you brought. There are other family members on different parts of the mountain with their own perspective and perception of the problems. And you know that you're so close to the rock that it's darn near impossible to have a completely objective perspective.

Tied to the other end of your rope (there are strings attached, ya know) is your spouse. Your spouse may be right next to you or a hundred feet above or below you, but one thing you can count on for sure is that his or her perspective of the family problem will be different from yours, just like everyone else on that rock.

Your goal as a couple is not to have the same perspective because different perspectives are essential to a healthy marriage. Though you may agree with your spouse on a number of issues, your perspective is yours and yours alone. Your perspective is your vantage point for your eyes, heart, and mind.

The goal is to be on common ground with your husband or wife regarding how you choose to respond to extended family problems. Couples can waste huge amounts of energy by going to extremes against one another over issues that aren't always theirs. If you want to have a better, happier marriage, here are some solid handholds to hang on to—

Stay Tied into Your Spouse. Untie from your spouse while the storms are brewing and you will reap the whirlwind. Your first loyalty, that commitment you made when you were first married, is to your spouse. According to God's Word, you untied from your family just as your spouse untied from his or her family. You both agreed to love, listen, and support one another first before anyone else. You have left and cleft. When conflict occurs, especially when you don't agree with your spouse, it's tempting to side with your family. This is particularly true in families where there are in-law conflicts. Is it surprising, then, when one spouse who feels rejected says to the other, *"You always take your family's side!"*?

Stay Out of Your Family's Problems. This should be a no-brainer, but think of how many people you know who create their own problems by getting involved in family problems that are none of their business. Sounds weird, but some people get a kick out of conflict. If things get a bit boring in the family, what better way to get some attention than getting everyone else all riled up?

Just because there's a problem somewhere in your family tree does not mean it's your problem. Especially if you haven't been invited. And then, even if you do get a phone call or a letter from another family member asking for your advice or allegiance, think twice before jumping in the ring.

Let other family members resolve their own conflicts. No yeah-buts about it. In cases where there's any type of abuse or severe marriage troubles, it is important for family to step in and hold others accountable, but even that needs to be done with great caution and sensitivity. You and your spouse are wise to spend your best energies sharpening your own marriage.

Watch Your Words. It's been said that an enemy stabs you in the back and a friend stabs you in front. I'd venture to say that nobody knows where to stab you better than your own family. It may be easy to blow off an unkind comment or insult from those outside your family, but mean and malicious words from family members have a tough time sliding off the meanest of alligator skins. Cruel words stick like superglue. Promise together with your spouse to refuse to participate in family gossip, rumors, lies, and insults. Stand tall above the dangerous cesspool of gossip that breeds mistrust and suspicion. Even if one or more family members are blatantly wrong on an issue, "discussing it" behind their backs does not solve the problem and usually creates a bigger one. Like shouts from a mountaintop, unkind words can echo back and forth in a person's heart long after the initial words are spoken.

Don't allow extended family problems to knock your marriage off common ground. Your first priority is your marriage, and no matter how tempting it might be to jump into a juicy family feud, back out and stay out. Don't mistake age for maturity. Sometimes, the best thing you can do for fighting family members is to let them figure out their own messes. The actions, attitudes, and behavior patterns of your parents, stepparents, in-laws, or siblings may never change, but the one thing you can change *that will have a definite positive effect in your marriage* is how you and your spouse choose to stay apart from it and stick together. Staying on common ground is a whole lot better than getting stuck on a cliff.

Your Hair Looks —Uh—Different

29

I had some words with my wife and
she had some paragraphs with me.
—Fearful Anonymous Husband

guys are often accused by women of being poor communicators. Some women also contend that practically everything that
comes out of a guy's mouth is wrong. That's an extreme I'm
not sure most guys can accept. But I must confess that history
is in women's favor when it comes to *"D'oh!"* statements made
by men.

In the attempt to show their intellectual prowess and
visionary thinking, some of our greatest world leaders, inven-
tors, and business leaders have said things that made them look
downright foolish a few years later. Look at what these brilliant
men did to insert a size ten foot into a size three mouth—

> **"Drill for oil? You mean drill into the ground
> to try and find oil? You're crazy."**
> Drillers whom Edwin L. Drake tried to enlist
> to his project to drill for oil in 1859

"Louis Pasteur's theory of germs is ridiculous fiction."
Pierre Pachet, Professor of Physiology at Toulouse, 1872

"This 'telephone' has too many shortcomings to be
seriously considered as a means of communication.
The device is inherently of no value to us."
Western Union internal memo, 1876

"Heavier-than-air flying machines are impossible."
Lord Kelvin, president, Royal Society, 1895

"There is no reason anyone would want a computer
in their home."
Ken Olson, president, chairman, and founder
of Digital Equipment Corp., 1977

"640K ought to be enough for anybody."
Bill Gates

"Gee, honey, your hair looks—uh—different."
Deceased husband whose death remains a mystery

Okay, guys can say some pretty dumb things, but look at how often they are set up for failure by their wives. What is a guy really supposed to say when his wife asks him what he thinks of her hair? If he likes her hair, great, but if not, then what? Most guys, if they're honest, really don't understand the hair and nail thing.

I live in San Clemente, California, which is right next to the Camp Pendleton Marine Base. Consequently, as you can imagine, San Clemente is filled with enough barbershops to shave all the heads of the entire Pacific Fleet. I can get in and out of the chair in a few minutes for seven bucks. My barber's name, you've guessed correctly, is Butch (I'm serious), and all Butch needs to do to save me time and money is to get his sheep-shearing buzz trimmer and have at it. I'm outta there in no time looking like a new recruit. By the time I get back to the house, I'm ready to hear my wife greet me in a sultry voice, "Hey, soldier—I like a man in a uniform."

More than a few husbands have wondered why their wives have to pay tons of money and waste productive sunlight hours by getting their hair trimmed, weaved, styled, colored, crimped, washed, waxed, and sealed. These same guys ask, Why can't women just get buzz haircuts? Why don't women show their solidarity with the young men who protect and serve our country? Come on, if Demi Moore can be a Navy SEAL and get her hair buzzed, my wife can too!

Guys, I'm gonna let you in on a little secret: Women like to get their hair and nails done because of what it does for them *emotionally*. Now this isn't necessarily a bad thing, but it is just another one of those unfathomable female mysteries guys like you and me will never completely understand. When we get our hair cut, we are just a piece of meat buzzing through the barber's butcher saw so he can move on to the next guy. We suffer indignities and verbal abuse when our barber barks at us when he's done, "Now get outta my chair you slob, I gotta living to make! *NEXT!*"

For women, the hair and nail thing is completely the opposite experience. It goes something like this—

Women, particularly moms, spend the majority of their day waiting on their children. If a guy is really, really lucky, she waits on him too. Women who work in the marketplace have double duties with professional and home responsibilities. A woman who's a professional mom is faced with a full plate of nonstop cleaning, carpooling, making meals, bathing, playing with and disciplining children, going to the grocery store, and just about every other little task you can imagine. By the end of the day or week, she is fried and ready for a break.

Then the phone rings.

It's one of her girlfriends who asks her if she wants to get her hair and nails done tomorrow. Your wife leaps at the chance and responds with a resounding "Yes!"

After making arrangements for a baby-sitter, she leaves her crying children who are clawing at her legs and inflicting fear of abandonment issues on her, heads for the hair salon, and sits down in the chair next to her friend.

For the next few hours, your wife is in pure heaven. She has nothing to worry about. No one to take care of. No breaking up fights or trying to balance the checkbook. She doesn't have to think about pleasing you or anyone else, and what a wonderful feeling that is.

All the care and attention are focused on *her*. She is being pampered, nurtured, and cared for. The mood in the hair salon is relaxing, and as her hair is being washed with shampoo and warm water, she feels all that stress of her hectic schedule flow right down the drain. The stylist has washed her hair, massaged her shoulders, and asked how she'd like her hair cut or colored, and most important, her friend has listened to her feelings about how she's doing, what's happening in her home, her marriage, her kids' lives.

When she's done with her hair and nails, she feels rejuvenated, relaxed, pampered, and pretty. If she has time, she'll grab a quick lunch with her friend. There, they'll talk more about their lives, their feelings, and what's important to them. By the end of the day, your wife feels like a new woman, and she's ready to have her children and husband run into her arms telling her how much they've missed her and how pretty her new haircut looks.

The kids always do their part right? But the husbands!?

Guys, if your wife asks you, "How do you like my new haircut?" don't react as if you've just bumped into the bride of Frankenstein. This will not endear your wife to you. Even though this is another one of those no-win questions that guys usually miserably fail at, don't get that deer-in-the-headlights look on your face and stutter like a blubbering idiot. Whatever you do, don't react with any of the following misguided statements—

You paid seventy-five bucks for THAT?

I like it better the way you had it before.

You didn't get electrocuted, did you?

You got your hair cut? Really?

Cindy Crawford doesn't do her hair like that!

Butch could've done it for seven bucks.

Unless you're seriously thinking about committing hairy-kairy, don't even think of commenting negatively about your wife's hair. Why? you ask. You thought marriage was supposed to be about honesty and truth-telling, right? It is, but let me ask you this: Are you willing to die over fallen hair follicles? Learn a lesson from my friends at Camp Pendleton and choose your battles wisely!

What you're actually paying for when your wife goes to get her hair and nails done is not the latest style or cuticle moistener. *You're paying for therapy.* Ask any woman how she feels about herself before she walks into a hair salon compared to how she feels when she walks out, and she'll tell you the difference is immeasurable.

Before, your wife walked into the hair salon feeling tired, emotionally exhausted, and sick of her hair; now she has returned home feeling refreshed and invigorated. She feels great about herself and wants to hear you extol and admire her beauty. Here is your chance to score major points by allowing her to bask in your affirmation and praise.

Don't mess it up, guys. If you do, you're going to be throwing all that therapy money right down the drain.

Now, pay attention. All you have to say is, *"WOW, you look great!"*

It's that simple. Memorize that line.

Of course, you never know, that line could backfire too.

Keep your guard up. Watch for swinging purses and the sound of your wife screaming, *"LIAR!"*

Common Ground

Words have such power. With a single word, glance, or facial expression, we can hurt our spouse's feelings without even meaning to. Though it's fun to laugh about the hair dilemmas almost every husband has had to face when asked how he likes his wife's hair, what's not funny is when couples intentionally use words to hurt one another.

That brings up another major difference between men and women. Guys are used to kidding each other and playing war-of-the-words one-upmanship. Ever since junior high school, guys have been into verbal king of the mountain sparring matches. It's that male, competitive, always-jockeying-for-position thing that women are not into. Unless they're losing it, guys just aren't very sensitive to things like hair. Women are.

For example, when I come home after getting a haircut from Butch, my head will look like it's been run through a compost mulcher. Krista will take one look at my hair, laugh, and say, "It'll look better after you take a shower." My feelings aren't hurt. She's right. It's happened enough times I know it's true. But—but—but, if I were to say that to her, I'd be sleeping in the backyard with the coyotes. Women care about what their husbands say about them. Joking about a woman's hair or looks is not a laughing matter.

If you want to establish a solid foundation for your marriage, get on the common ground of using words that build up your spouse. You have the capacity to build up your spouse's self-image by saying positive and kind words. When you deliberately say something unkind, you not only blow your spouse out of the water with a metaphorical torpedo, you also knock yourself off the common ground you share with your spouse.

Before you say or do something that would hurt your spouse's feelings, take a second and think about the consequences. How many simple disagreements turn into big arguments all because of one or two sharp, cutting words? What's to be gained by attacking your spouse's actions or character? Will sarcasm, nagging, ridicule, contempt, or cynicism help solve the problem?

Instead of lobbing verbal hand grenades at your spouse, make it your goal to control your tongue. When there's no conflict present, talk about how you both would like to be spoken to when you're in a disagreement. Make it a goal to say three or four nice things to your spouse each day. ("It's a beautiful day" doesn't count.)

It's simple. We need to tell our spouses what we like about them or something we appreciate about their personality or character. By using words that build up, motivate, and encourage them, we can leave them feeling refreshed, rejuvenated, and relaxed.

Even if they're having a bad hair day.

Who Wears the Pants?

30

Adam to Eve: Hey! I wear the plants in this family!

i give up. I'm whupped. I don't have the energy to try to wear the pants in my home anymore.

A few weeks ago, my wife brought home this list of twelve rules from her women's meeting at church. Every one of the 150 women in attendance received one. Now I understand how underground movements begin. This is the type of subversive material that is sneaking into homes across the nation as men pick their noses in traffic on the way to work.

It's really a brilliant piece. I wish I had thought of it, but writing a guys' version would have led to a new arms race. Read it over, guys, and let's face it—it's totally true.

We're whupped.

Ahem—The Rules

1. The FEMALE always makes the Rules.

2. The Rules are subject to change at any time without prior notification.

3. No MALE can possibly know all the Rules.

4. If the FEMALE suspects the MALE knows the Rules, she must immediately change some or all of the Rules.

5. The FEMALE is never wrong.

6. If the FEMALE is wrong it is because of a flagrant misunderstanding that was a direct result of something the MALE did or said.

7. If Rule #6 applies, the MALE must apologize immediately for causing the misunderstanding.

8. The FEMALE can change her mind at any time.

9. The MALE must never change his mind without the express written consent of the FEMALE.

10. The FEMALE has every right to be angry and upset at any time.

11. The MALE must remain calm at all times unless the FEMALE wants him to be angry and upset.

12. If the FEMALE has PMS, all Rules are null and void.

Women do make the rules and if you think I'm kidding, let's explore this reality a little more closely by looking at the following conundrums that leave men shaking their heads in confusion—

There's Been a Change in Plans. If a woman changes the plans for going out for the evening, it's because they're flexible, social, and thoughtful. (Note: All of these are positive-sounding words.) Her thinking goes something like this: "Oh, I forgot to tell you. I invited Steve and Denise to dinner with us tonight. It's been so long since we've seen them and I thought the four of us would have fun together."

As the guy, even if you have about as much in common with Steve and his wife as with a doorknob and a head of lettuce, you must shut up or risk causing a huge fight.

However, if *you* change the plans for the evening, you are now rude, insensitive, and uncaring (note: all negative-sounding words). For good measure, you're also a big jerk.

If you say the exact same words to your wife, "Oh, I forgot to tell you. I invited Steve and Denise to dinner with us tonight. It's been a long time since we've seen them and I thought the four of us would have fun together," then you'll get an earful of the following extreme—

"You did what? I thought we were going to have a romantic evening alone! You never want to go out with me by yourself; you're always bringing other people along. It would have been considerate of you to ask first!

"Now I've got to change my clothes. I don't want them to see me in this outfit. Now that I have to change, we're going to be late! *And*—the reason we haven't seen Steve and Denise for so long is that she's been talking behind my back.

"You and Steve are going to spend the whole night talking about work and sports, and I'm going to be stuck in my chair, pretending that I like the woman, listening to her blab on and on about how much weight she's lost and how much she loves her favorite fat-free cat food bars."

The Porsche Must Always Follow the Mercedes. Concerning sex, it's been said that men are Porsches and women are mercenaries, I mean, Mercedes. Though both cars are made by German manufacturers, one is always raring to go, but the other likes to warm its engine over conversation, a leisurely meal, a soft touch, the sharing of feelings, a warm embrace, some light kissing, new jewelry, an unlimited spending account at Nordstrom, tender words of affection, and an intimate setting to make the moment just right. Guys, any list that long is an official rule.

Women know that guys are Porsches that need sex more than food, water, or Monday Night Football. (Okay, I concede, for some guys that last point may be up for debate.) In general, though, a guy's gotta tail a Mercedes to get what he needs. Women use this extreme of male physiology to their advantage through the use of cunning psychology. If you've been married longer than your honeymoon, you know that psychology always wins over physiology.

Guys, you ain't making whoopee unless you've been whupped. The Porsche *always* follows the Mercedes. It's a rule and you know it. You can rev your engine to impress her, but if you really want her, you gotta stay in her lane.

You Need to Be the Spiritual Leader in This House. I don't know why God wanted men to be the spiritual leaders in homes, especially when a lot of guys can't even find the glasses on their heads. Yes, we know and have been told by our wives that men have the God-given responsibility to be spiritual leaders in the home, but let's be honest: How can a man be a spiritual leader if he's whupped? Would you take anyone seriously if the only thing he wore around the house was red boxer shorts? How is a guy supposed to take the lead when his woman is wearing his pants?

Common Ground

Power, position, and authority are at the heart of "The Rules." Ever since that debacle in the Garden of Eden, men have sought to rule over women and women have fought back with their own set of rules. Each side has gone to extremes attempting to achieve dominance over the other.

Wearing the pants is a question of dominance in the marriage relationship where it seems impossible for one size to fit all. It's only natural, when you don't freely receive from your spouse what you want and need in your marriage, to compete for it. This competition, battle, test of wills, call it what you will, leads to extremes.

Among guys generally, "Who wears the pants in your family?" is a question of power, position, and authority. Typically, the issue comes up when a guy is afraid to ask his wife if he can go bowling with his buddies. A guy also habitually ducks derogatory phrases like "wimp," "wuss," and "yellow-bellied chicken liver" that can damage the fragile male ego. Until a husband and wife have settled the issues of power and authority in their home, they'll find themselves splitting at the seams.

The dilemma of power, position, and authority in marriage is this: Guys are afraid of being pulled down and women are scared of being kept down. In other words, there's only one pair of pants in a marriage and two people with very separate and distinct wills are trying to hop in 'em.

If a woman wears the pants in the family, her husband hates to be seen as a browbeaten, henpecked worm of a man who snaps to attention whenever he hears the whistle blow. If a man wears the pants in the family, his wife is afraid of being perceived as a mute, unproductive invertebrate whose whole identity is wrapped up in the dominating father figure she married because she was completely incapable of taking care of herself. Sounds a bit extreme, doesn't it?

This tug of war is heavily influenced by our culture. For decades, men and women have followed all sorts of culturally influenced messages that have led to extremes in marriage. Men have been told to "take charge" as the head of the household, and women have been told to "submit, submit, submit." Well, we all know that many women have challenged the culture by saying, "Forget it. I'm not submitting to that lughead. *Let him peel my grapes.*"

Despite what some people think, the Bible has a completely different take on power, position, and authority. It works like this: First, both husband and wife are told to "submit to one another out of reverence for Christ" (Ephesians 5:21). God said it—it's not just a woman's job to submit. If a marriage is going to grow, be nourished, and prosper on common ground, you and your spouse need to submit to each other. That simply means serving your spouse before yourself by putting your spouse's needs, wants, and desires before your own. I know, easier said than done.

Second, women are told to submit to their husbands as the church submits itself to Christ, and men are told to love their wives sacrificially as Christ loved the church. Guys, that means we gotta die. If you're the head of the household and your faith is as authentic as you say it is, step right up to that chopping block. If you're truly dead, your wife will have no problem submitting to you. Another benefit of being dead is that you don't have to worry about "The Rules."

This whole idea of submitting to one another works best if you're both on common ground about who wears the pants. If the answer isn't clear enough by now, you both wear the pants. One of you gets the "Submit Leg #1" and the other of you gets the "Submit Leg #2." Your mutual submission to one another will reflect the true character of your commitment to God. God knows you both have wills to contend with, so instead of going to extremes, you can hem in a lot of hassles by not trying to pull a power trip on your partner. Instead of dominating, serve your spouse in love. One size can fit all if you're willing to be stretched.

Nobody Likes Change but a Wet Baby

31

All perfect marriages are made up of couples who accept the fact that they have an imperfect marriage.

ever since my wife threw up in my lap on our honeymoon, I have been in charge of cleaning up every bodily fluid in our home that doesn't quite make it to the potty or sink on time. *Except for sweat.*

Call me "Captain Bio," "Mr. Hazardous Materials," "The Grand Pooh-Bah of the Potty Patrol." I wipe, swipe, mop, swab, scoop, shovel, hose, and Shopvac any bodily fluid that can be produced by a human orifice. I've told my wife a million times that mine is a stinky job and we should unite forces in battling biological warfare. She pooh-poohs that idea and hands me a bucket. Krista says I should clean up all things offensive because I'm the man of the house. That's sexist. She says it's one of the privileges of having a home office.

It all started early one morning on a bus ride back to Barfalona, I mean, Barcelona, Spain. Krista and I had just spent a couple of nights at a little pension along Spain's Costa Azul. In order to get back to Barcelona, we had to catch a bus at 7:00 A.M.

Waking up late, we awkwardly jogged and lugged our heavy backpacks to the bus stop. Out of breath, with sweat dripping from our brows in the early morning Spanish sun, we powered down a quick breakfast of water and a couple of oranges before boarding the bus filled with Spanish vacationers.

As the happy honeymooners settled into their seats while the bus accelerated down the beautiful coastline, the asphalt road started to S W E R V E. Like a ferocious herd of Pamplona bulls chasing a flock of flamenco dancers, el agua and las naranjas launched a gastrointestinal stampede.

"Ja-Ja-Joey . . . I'm not feeling very good."

Uh-oh, I thought. *Her stomach's doing the macarena. What should I do?*

"Hurry," Krista pleaded. "Get something . . . a bag . . . a cup . . . anything!"

I desperately looked around the seat, in my knapsack, the seat pouch in front of me. No bolsas. Nada. Only the newest version of Murphy's Law, "Barf Bags Are Only Available When Not Needed." Ay caramba! I couldn't find anything worthy of sustaining a major wave of instant liquid breakfast. Desperate, I looked in my knapsack again and pulled out a pathetic little tourista map. With holes in it.

"Here . . . here . . ." I winced with a whimper. "Use this."

That's all my bride needed as she leaned over my lap and emptied her stomach contents. The clear, watery, orange-laced emesis (English translation: barf, yak, or vomit) roared into and straight through the holes in the map just southwest of Madrid. It flowed through my fingers, onto my lap, over the seat, and onto the floor.

The rain in Spain does not flow mainly on the plain.

As the bus downshifted up a hill, Krista's breakfast streamed to the back of the bus. Cruising down the next hill, *el barfo* flowed to the front of the bus. Hushed, urgent alarms of "Vomita! Vomita!" sounded behind and in front of us as perturbed Spaniards cast snarling glances at the newlywed gringos.

"Oh, I feel much better now," Krista chirped and laughed at the sight of my wet seat, soggy Levi's, and wilted map.

"Gross. Completely foul negative," I moaned, wiping my hands on my jeans.

In our premarital counseling, there was nothing, absolutely nothing said about who could barf on whom and who had to clean it up! When we stood at the altar, we said, "For better or for worse," not "For better or for barf." That was the simple, disgusting beginning of my humble role as our family's "Chief Biological Engineer."

If you haven't chucked this book out the window or in the toilet yet, I can tell we are potty pals. I'm the first to admit there aren't many books that deal with such sensitive scatological subject matter in a spiritual light. (For you germ freaks, don't worry . . . this chapter has been sanitized for your protection.) If you're a bit offended by all this American Standard talk, I'll wave my bio banner high 'cause you can't fool me. I know what happens in your home: DOODOO-CACA-PEEPEE-POOPOO. Whether you're a mom or dad dealing with daily diaper dilemmas, I feel your potty pain.

You're attempting to toilet-train your toddler and you wish you could get frequent-flier miles for using the word *almost.*

Your seven-year-old Indian Guide pounds down four donuts and three cups of red bug juice at the Tribal Powwow. Later, around 2:00 A.M., he enters elaborate initiation rites battling the evil stomach spirits before he fails to complete his journey of worship before the Great White Porcelain god.

You enter the nursery and discover there is a new artist in the family using you-know-what for finger paint!

If your guy is whining about wiping up Number 1 or Number 2, I don't feel sorry for him one bit. Grab a bucket, pal. If I can be Mr. Barforama, so can you. If you're facing a major diaper dilemma, just get yourself one of those Ebola outfits and use a lot of wipes.

If you're a woman and you've got the bio blues, you gotta understand that even though guys effortlessly burp and pass gas stronger than your average hurricane, they're still a bit clueless when it comes to dirty work. Guys aren't quick to understand that there's meaning in that mess on the carpet. Yes, *there is meaning in that mess.* A verse in Proverbs loosely translated reads, "If the ox is in the barn, so is the dung." Whatever that mess is, that mess is a sign of life. Call it divine waste management. A creation of creation. A holy pile. Smelly, yes, but dare we say from the hand of God?

Let's be honest for a moment and do away with our sanitized, Protecto-covered understanding of faith and Scripture. A quick glance and the Bible is anything but squeaky clean. Where was Jesus born? What did Mary's labor and delivery room smell like? Jesus is called what? The Good Shepherd. Ever caught a whiff of sheep?

Oh, I know nobody is thinking such deep thoughts when they're delirious from lack of sleep after being up all night with a sick child. I certainly don't. I'm guilty too. I grump and groan. Captain Bio does not always carry a smile and relish his role. Yeah, it's a smelly job and someone's got to do it, but when I enter my kids' rooms late at night and smell that thick, sweet, warm, heavy breath with every rise and fall of their little chests, I receive a little grace called perspective and that's all I need. I wouldn't trade those oh-so-nasty bodily fluids for the world.

Common Ground

I'll be the first to admit that my wife changes the vast majority of diapers in our home, and ever since our first daughter was born, the one thing we've both discovered is that nobody likes change but a wet baby.

About the only stable thing you can count on in marriage is change. Change is what leads couples to extremes as each person tries to cope with the inherent stress and pressure that come with change. If you're not careful, too much change will knock you and your spouse off common ground. And change is what it will take to get you back on common ground.

It doesn't matter if you've been married for five days, five years, fifteen years, or fifty years, change in marriage is inevitable. Nothing stays static in this world. You change. Your spouse changes. Your children change. Your job changes. Your friends change. Your circumstances change. Your family changes. Successful marriages are those that refuse to allow changes and circumstances to erode the common ground upon which the marriage grows and flourishes.

When you and your spouse are going through changes, particularly difficult transitions like a move, a job loss, or a death in the family, it's tempting to want to hole up inside yourself and pull away from your spouse. What's crucial during this time, though, is to have clear and consistent communication with one another. Don't allow change to eat away the common ground that keeps you together. Lean into God and lean into one another through sharing your thoughts and feelings, hopes and fears, dreams and goals. Do this and the common ground you share together will stand fast against the storm. And if you're not facing any major changes or storms right now, get ready because they always appear when you least expect them.

When I was thirty years old, I lost a job I loved due to a building campaign at a church where I worked for seven years. When I worked at the church, people asked me what I liked best about my job. Without question, my response was always, "I love being on staff. I love working with people and I love working with the people on staff. They are fun, supportive, and great to be around—I couldn't ask for a better place to serve."

When I was let go, it felt like I'd been kicked in the teeth. For me, it was like getting booted off the team. Growing up, I'd always been on sports teams and I prided myself on being a team player. In college, I played Division I volleyball and was assistant coach to a women's volleyball team that won a national championship. After college, I traveled to South America with Athletes in Action to coach a volleyball team. Never before had I been kicked off a team. Team loyalty ran thicker in my blood than plasma.

Now, I was off the team and out of a job. I was hurt, angry, humiliated, and scared.

Call it a defining moment in my life.

Krista just so happened to be eight months pregnant with Ellie, our second child, and I was beginning a Ph.D. program in the fall and had no clue how I was going to pay for it. When Ellie was born, she and we spent a week in intensive care for the breathing problems she was having. Two months later, I developed chronic tendonitis in both wrists, which is a wicked stepchild to carpal tunnel syndrome. For a writer, this is the voodoo-like equivalent of some unseen evil person pushing hot, sharp pins into your fingers and wrists every time you sit down at the keyboard. Four years later, I'm still praying for these blazing thorns to be yanked outta my flesh.

Three years of job changes, financial struggles, grief over losing my job, confusion about my future, and chronic health problems led me into a spiritual wasteland of doubt, apathy, anger, and depression. Our premarital counselor never prepared me for any of this! Like a wet baby, I was crying for someone to change me and my circumstances. But who wants to change a thirty-something guy wearing *Depends?*

Through all these problems, I've discovered a few things that I'm grateful haven't changed. First, the author of all change, God Himself, does not change or cease to be with us when we're going through the painful changes in life that come our way. He is always faithful, always loving, always caring, and always forgiving. Even when my wrists are on fire, I have the unconditional promise of His presence.

The second thing I discovered that didn't change was the love of my wife. We have spent many long nights the past four years pouring out our hearts to each other and the Lord. I've been through more than enough extremes as I've shared my greatest frustrations and fears with Krista. She has been a constant source of strength and encouragement when I've felt as though my feet were firmly planted in midair.

What also didn't change was the love and support of my family and close friends. Thickheaded guy that I am, I discovered that they still liked me for who I was and not what I did. It didn't matter if I was a youth minister, a regular work guy, a starving author, or future telecommunications mogul; they liked me for being just me.

When you and your spouse are experiencing the extreme pain that comes from sudden and unexpected changes in your lives, the strongest assets you have are the three Fs: Faith, Family, and Friends. That's what matters most in the short life you live. That, and a miracle or two, is just about all you need to weather the stormy changes that come your way. Like changing a wet baby, life is sometimes messy, but it's worth the labor of love.

Hand Me That Remote!

32

A man has at most seven items in his bathroom—a toothbrush, toothpaste, shaving cream, razor, shampoo, a bar of soap, and a towel from the Holiday Inn.

The average number of items in a typical woman's bathroom is 437. A man would not be able to identify most of these items.

In the days of old, kings had scepters, shepherds had staffs, and warriors had swords. Today, guys have the remote. It is one of the last remaining symbols of power and authority a guy can get a grip on. So men and women often go to extremes over who has control of the remote.

Like other extreme themes we've examined in this book so far, the remote control is (guess again) *a control issue.* Step into any home across America and you're likely to hear a battle taking place by remote control—

HUSBAND: Let's see what's on ESPN. *[Click!]*

WIFE: No, wait! I like that old movie!

HUSBAND: We can come back to it. Bummer, Utah lost. *[Click!]*

WIFE: Okay, hand me that remote. Let's go back to my show. Oh no—not *Baywatch*! Gimme that thing!

HUSBAND: Your show? I'm the one holding "The Dictator." *[Click!]* All right! It's *The Three Stooges*!

WIFE: We always watch what you want to watch!

HUSBAND: That's because whoever has "The Dictator" is The Dictator. Besides, we watched that dumb romance last night. *[Click!]*

WIFE: That was a beautiful story! At least until you started snoring. You know I hate WWF wrestling! Now hand me that remote!

HUSBAND: Let me just check one more channel. I wanna see if that motorcycle chase is still on the news. *[Click!]*

WIFE: Why can't you stick to one channel? Why are all you men afraid of commitment?

HUSBAND: We like to keep our options and channels open. *[Click! Click!]*

WIFE: Well, here's an option for you buddy: Either you give me that remote or I'm gonna wrestle you to the ground, hogtie you like a sow, and force you to watch the Home Shopping Network.

HUSBAND: Okay, okay, I give up. Anything, but that! *[Click! Click! Click! Click!]*

A recent *Los Angeles Times* article explored a number of fascinating insights describing the differences between men's and women's television viewing habits. I don't know what those researchers were thinking, but was it any surprise to discover that the number one show for men in America was Monday Night Football? Was it really a shocking surprise to learn that Monday Night Football didn't make the Top 20 list for women? How many thousands of dollars were wasted on a discovery that the general public already knows?

Is it any wonder there are two to three televisions in every home?

Men and women are different!

Battling over the remote is just another down-home Americana example of how women are always right and men are never wrong. Women always pick the right television shows where relationships are developed, and men never pick television shows that make no logical sense. Women know they possess the intelligence, powers of reason, and concentration skills to watch a television show, including commercials, for two hours straight. Men know they are wired for action and that they can adeptly follow seventeen shows at once by clicking the remote at the slightest glimpse of a commercial.

Women are faithfully committed to watching their favorite show on time every week for however long their favorite show is on the air. This example of commitment is something most women think guys are not capable of, but that's not true. A guy will stay committed to his favorite show as long as that show ends with, "Same Bat Time, Same Bat Channel." Guys can be as faithful as The Boy Wonder.

Women and men haven't always gone to extremes over the remote. Before the remote was invented, men and women were on an even playing field for station identification. Whoever wanted to change the channel had to be motivated enough to get up, walk over, and flip the channel on the TV set. If one spouse wanted to guard their favorite program, that meant they had to watch it standing up. When the remote came along, the defensive strategies changed. The defensive spouse could now hide the remote under the couch, sit on it in the La-Z-Boy, or run around the room channel-surfing from any chosen strategic position.

Before the remote, guys didn't have the coach potato potbellies that are so prevalent today. No remote meant that guys got plenty of exercise. Want to change the channel? A guy had to stand up, stretch, scratch, walk over, bend over, flip the channel, stand up straight, walk back to the couch, and sit back down. Over the course of an entire evening, a guy might do that forty or fifty times. A workout like that five nights a week and a guy was prepared to run a marathon.

What further complicates the remote dilemma is when there's only one TV in a home with satellite television. This is when men and women really go to extremes. It's one thing to operate a remote for cable television or the VCR, but operating a satellite television is a whole different ball game. Satellite television is the big leagues of remote control. Only experienced channel surfers need apply.

Five hundred-plus channels mean a lot of choices, and a lot of choices mean a lot of potential conflict. If a guy wants to watch the Autobahn Accident Channel or the running of the bulls in Pamplona or Scottish caber tossing and that conflicts with his wife's wish to watch a Turkish soap opera or an Eskimo cooking class or Michael Bolton Live from the United Republic of Lounge Lizards, then there's going to be a serious two-outta-three round of paper, rock, scissors to see who gets the remote.

With satellite television, you just don't click and go to another channel. Some clicks require planetary realignment, a thorough knowledge of GPS (global positioning systems), and a few basic meteorological skills. The worldwide TV guide that comes with satellite television is as thick as a phone book, and you have to take a six-week class to figure out how to use it. All of this can be very frustrating to first-time users, especially couples who are still arguing over who gets the remote. For this reason, I don't recommend couples getting satellite television within the first few years of marriage. There are too many confusing control issues to work through.

Common Ground

It's obvious that you and I can't press a button and expect our spouse to immediately click into our deepest needs, wants, dreams, and desires for our lives or our marriage. Marriage by remote control does not work. You can't turn your marriage on and off with the flip of a button. Marriage is a whole lot more work than that. Especially in those times when you are tired, frustrated, irritated with your husband or wife, disappointed over unmet expectations, and really ticked off at the extremes you and your spouse go to in order to get each other's attention.

We've talked a lot about what it takes for you and your spouse to get on common ground to create a truly great marriage, but there's one more thought I want to leave you with: *Common ground is holy ground.*

Every love relationship begins on the common ground of mutual attraction, shared interests, likes and dislikes, dreams, goals, and desires. The moment you exchanged vows with your spouse that common ground became holy ground because God designed marriage to be an extraordinary relationship. And anything God gets intimately involved with automatically becomes holy. It's not a complicated idea. Really.

Getting on common ground when you were dating or first married was easy; staying on common ground in your marriage for the long haul is hard work filled with wonderful highs and discouraging lows. That's what this book has been all about: *finding the common ground in your marriage without going to extremes and remembering that the common ground you and your spouse stand on is still holy ground.*

I have a sneaking suspicion that when we get our marriages back on common ground instead of resorting to the knee-jerk reaction of going to extremes, then we will be in a better position to understand and live by God's design for marriage. God deals in marriage futures. He is serious about couples staying together for life. Call His position extreme, but it's the principles found in the Bible that give husbands and wives what they need to live unselfish lives. His principles will give you the strength and direction you need for thinking of your spouse before yourself. Resist the temptation to give in to the forces in your life that can pull your marriage off common ground. Don't allow your choices, your schedule, your work, your children, your friends, your finances, your in-laws, your expectations, or your other commitments to pull you away from your most important earthly relationship.

And even when you and your spouse go to extremes (and you *will* go to extremes), common ground is the place where you can meet your mate through offering each other healthy doses of compassion and forgiveness. You can make your marriage a great marriage if you're willing to invest your best time, energy, and attention. All great adventures are high challenges filled with risks and rewards. They can also be a lot of fun, and that's what I hope you find in this wild, extreme, crazy commitment called marriage.

Though it's sometimes a fierce tug of war, fight to make your marriage a great marriage. Focus on the basics. Love, support, and serve your spouse as if this were your last day on earth. Do these things extremely well, and you'll discover that when you're on common ground, it doesn't really matter who's always right or who's never wrong. All that matters is that you're both standing together on common ground. *Holy ground*.

And that's the way marriage is meant to be.